ON
WRITING

Also by George V. Higgins

The Friends of Eddie Coyle, 1972

The Digger's Game, 1973

Cogan's Trade, 1974

A City on a Hill, 1975

The Friends of Richard Nixon, 1975

The Judgment of Deke Hunter, 1976

Dreamland, 1977

A Year or So with Edgar, 1979

Kennedy for the Defense, 1980

The Rat on Fire, 1981

The Patriot Game, 1982

A Choice of Enemies, 1984

Style Vs. Substance, 1984

Penance for Jerry Kennedy, 1985

Impostors, 1986

Outlaws, 1987

The Sins of the Fathers, 1988 (UK only)

Wonderful Years, Wonderful Years, 1988

The Progress of the Seasons, 1989

Trust, 1989

George V.
Higgins

On
Writing

Advice for Those Who Write
to Publish (or Would Like To)

HENRY HOLT AND COMPANY
New York

Published by Henry Holt and Company, Inc.,
115 West 18th Street, New York, New York, 10011.
Published in Canada by Fitzhenry & Whiteside Limited,
195 Allstate Parkway, Markham, Ontario L3R 4T8.

LIBRARY OF CONGRESS CATALOGING-IN-PUBLICATION DATA

Higgins, George V., 1939–
On writing : advice for those who write to publish (or would like to) / by George
V. Higgins.—1st ed.
    p.   cm.
ISBN 0-8050-1180-3
1. Authorship.   I. Title.
PN151.H54   1990
808′ .02—dc20   89-28808
                                                                    CIP

Henry Holt books are available at special discounts for bulk purchases for
sales promotions, premiums, fund-raising, or educational use. Special editions or book excerpts can also be created to specification.

For details contact:
Special Sales Director
Henry Holt and Company, Inc.
115 West 18th Street
New York, New York 10011

First Edition

Designed by Kathryn Parise

Printed in the United States of America
Recognizing the importance of preserving the written word,
Henry Holt and Company, Inc., by policy, prints all of its first
editions on acid-free paper. ∞
10   9   8   7   6   5   4   3   2   1

The following pages of acknowledgments constitute an ex-
tension of this copyright page.

ACKNOWLEDGMENTS

Grateful acknowledgment is made for permission to reprint the following: Excerpts from *A Farewell to Arms* by Ernest Hemingway, copyright 1929 by Charles Scribner's Sons, renewal copyright © 1957 by Ernest Hemingway, reprinted with permission of Charles Scribner's Sons, an imprint of Macmillan Publishing Company; "Silent Season of a Hero" from *Fame and Obscurity* by Gay Talese, permission granted by Gay Talese; excerpts from *Goodbye, Darkness: A Memoir of the Pacific War* by William Manchester, copyright © 1979, 1980 by William Manchester, by permission of Little, Brown and Company; "The Girls in Their Summer Dresses," from *Five Decades of Short Stories* by Irwin Shaw, copyright © 1937, '38, '39, '40, '41, '42, '43, '44, '45, '46, '47, '49, '50, '52, '53, '54, '55, '56, '57, '58, '61, '62, '63, '64, '67, '68, '69, '71, '73, '77, '78 by Irwin Shaw, reprinted by permission of Delacorte, a division of Bantam, Doubleday, Dell Publishing Group, Inc.; "Appearances" from *The Cape Cod Lighter* by John O'Hara, copyright © 1961, 1962 by John O'Hara, reprinted by permission of Random House, Inc.; excerpts from *Some Sort of Epic Grandeur* by Matthew Bruccoli, copyright © 1981 by Matthew Bruccoli, reprinted by permission of Harcourt Brace Jovanovich, Inc.; "You Could Look It Up" from *My World and Welcome to It* by James Thurber, copyright © 1942 by James Thurber, copyright © 1970 by Helen Thurber and Rosemary A. Thurber, permission granted by Harcourt Brace Jovanovich, Inc.; excerpts from *The Late George Apley: A Novel in the Form of a Memoir* by John P. Marquand, copyright 1936,

ON
WRITING

1

If you haven't always been doing it, you haven't always wanted to do it.

Edmund Wilson wrote a great deal. Most of his writing can be safely cited as explaining and eminently justifying his reputation as the leading American literary critic of this century. He had: a sharp mind; a generally foul disposition; no patience whatsoever for any kind of shilly-shallying, mushy thinking, or wishy-washy whining; and utter disdain, verging on contempt, for any hurt his harsh words might cause. In other words he was born to be a literary critic, there being in his lifetime (1895–1972) few attractive employment opportunities in the U.S. for professional torturers.

Since the first act of any prudent warrior is to acquire knowledge as complete as possible of the nature of his enemy; since every writer, by the agreement to be published, undertakes to provoke the serried critics at the hazard of their wrath; and since Wilson was so ferocious a paradigm of that often-scornful school, it is appropriate for the unblooded volunteer to consider Wilson's attitude on the general subject of writing—it implies the probable consequence to the writer of any show of weakness, self-pity, or indulgence: public ridicule.

The public at first usually does not honorably attack under the flag of critics' regiment. The first damage is done by one sapper or a single sniper, detached for duty from a loosely organized band of saboteurs, actual gender, age, and name uncertain; clandestine cover occupation: editor, taciturn and overworked; method of expressing rotten attitude: laconic, by printed, brief, rejection slip, stinging ridicule implicit; effect on victim: often crippling, self-diagnosed as "temporary writer's block," can be fatal, self-diagnosed as "permanent writer's block."

A shorter name, and a better one, for that condition, whether transient or perpetual, is "fear." And that is what Wilson cruelly suggested when he sneered at all its sufferers pitiably moaning: There's no such thing as writer's block—writers write; it's that simple. If the postulant's determination to be a writer is unequal to assault by either the fear of a first rejection, by that critic in camouflage, or proves inadequate to overcome the paralyzing fear of all rejections which that first one can bring about, so that the aspiring scribbler never makes that first submission, then that novice is not a writer and will never become one. There is no real poultice of compassion that will make the victim whole. If you do not seek to publish what you have written, then you are not a writer and you never will be.

Given the stern realities that hedge with thorns the inviting pastures that the few actual writers browse, it is useful before attempting to gain entrance to think about why on earth anyone would want to do a fool thing like that. With but very few exceptions, every writer whose published work you have read and relished managed to capture your attention only after taking a fearsome beating of the ego. In virtually every case, a dispassionate observer knowing all of the seemingly newly minted writer's record of depressing individual indentured servitude would conclude that he suffered from an insatiable masochistic appetite. The success of *The Friends of Eddie Coyle* was termed "overnight" in several quarters; that was one hell of a damned long night, lasting seventeen years and disgorging (along with dozens of stories, fewer than ten published; most for payment in copies of the magazines, none purchased for more than one hundred dollars) fourteen previous "novels," none of them ever accepted for publication, each of them rejected by at least five or six "reputable" but cold-blooded publishers on both sides of the Atlantic—in retrospect: thank God—and all of them hunted down and destroyed by their author after *Coyle* came out.

It takes most a while to learn enough about this trade to accomplish even the most modest of successes; those few who gain public notice in early youth with seeming ease are the beneficiaries of a whimsical fortune that almost never lasts long enough to get them successfully through completion of a third book contract. The odds against prevailing and surviving in the trade are mountainous: my guess is that the 624 young men listed on the rosters of North American major league baseball franchises at the start of each season have a mathematically better chance of success than the few rookie writers promoted each year—and those ballplayers represent only .0000024 percent of the American population. My guess is that in any given year, fewer Americans can manage to support themselves and their families solely on their earnings as professional free-lance writers than the 535 men and women whose tenacity and hard work have brought them the reward of trying to subsist on the salaries paid to members of the U.S. Senate and House of Representatives. By no means all of the nation's 750,000 or so lawyers crave elevation to the 761 judgeships authorized by Congress to serve on all the courts of the United States, from district to Supreme, but those who do in all likelihood face less intimidating odds than would dissuade the writer toiling in obscurity, if he only had some sense. None of those other covetable positions, nor those in medicine, teaching, science, the military, manufacturing, finance, media, or any other field—even entertainment and the performing arts—attracting the ambitious and talented, offers less in the nature of support and instruction to its raw volunteers.

And, where writing is concerned, it is seldom that a mentor can be found who is inclined and qualified to nudge the neophyte along; the development of a writer is usually too singular and individual for improvement without simultaneous damage by even the most sensitive overseer. When those rare occasions of such felicity occur, the overseer seldom wields much transferable power to secure the publication of the protégé—Fitzgerald's European discovery of Hemingway, leading to his energetic sponsorship of his later ungrateful rival in America, is one of few that come to mind.

And then there is the matter of teaching people how to write, an exercise in hubris if ever there was one. Survivors of college and university writing courses and workshops, now engaged in leading them, are acutely and uneasily aware from their own studies that most of the writers we deem exemplars of late nineteenth-century and twentieth-century American fiction writers never bothered to complete requirements for the bachelor's degree. Plainly we do not write because we have been taught to write; too many have written quite unburdened by such baggage. But, if there is no reliable etiological link between the two activities, then what the hell's the point of assembling the hopefuls and studying the craft from the practitioner's point of view?

Efficiency, we hope; the person suffering from the benign neurosis that requires daily accommodation of two contradic-

4

tory urges—the eminently solitary impulsion to write and the importunate craving to show off, via publication of what has been written—can use all the guidance available to resolve the warring claims. Creative writing under that dispensation becomes something that can be learned, but only by people who happen to have been afflicted, or gifted, probably from birth, by an *obsessive* desire to tell stories, and someone who has some personal experience of the oddity, if the stars and planets are in felicitous conjunction, can sometimes help the postulant in that learning process.

I emphasize *obsessive* for a reason. The desire to tell stories is appallingly common, if not universally so. Were it not, there would be no jokes, no gossip, no newspapers, and no broadcast news. The talent for telling stories is parceled out more rarely, only now and then generously enough to qualify its recipient to satisfy the normal desire.

What distinguishes the writers of stories from the hearers of stories is not, as hearers often wistfully aver, that the writers have simply had more time to tell them, or that the hearers have "just never seemed to get around to it"; it is that the writers never had any choice in the matter, but *had* to write their stories if they were to have some peace of mind. And the hearers didn't. It is much the same sort of distinction that separates the ambidextrous—or, in my case, the ambi-clumsy—from the incurably left-handed and right-handed majority of the population (and I think it very likely that the usual explanation for ambidexterity—it posits an atypical equilibrium of the right and left hemispheres of the brain, neither the analytical left side nor the creative right side achieving normal dominance—accounts as well for the drive to write; the vast majority of writers that I know have very nearly equal proficiency with their right and left hands, and while many of us use reading glasses, almost all have acquired the prescriptions for them from doctors who expressed mild puzzlement that neither the right nor the left eye showed customary dominance). Kindhearted acquaintances have as tactfully as possible suggested that the scribbler at the podium ought to evince more compassion than seems to be conveyed by the statement "No, you haven't always wanted to write a book, because if you had, you would have done it." I disagree and remain unreconstructed. No kindness is done when someone who has never *had* to write is reassured that he is really a writer unannounced. It simply isn't so.

So the first of the prerequisites to successful commencement, pursuit, and completion of one's progress toward learning to be a writer is the importunate desire to do it. Writing is hard work. Only those more bothered by shirking it than doing it can ever succeed at it. And do not be misled: we are not talking about self-discipline here, the exercise of will to overbear conflicting, distracting desires, but its antithesis: the overmastering desire to write that makes all other occupations and delights at best irritating nuisances and at worst infuriating acts of meddlesome interference. Jean-Baptiste Molière, another lawyer who went straight, disguised the nature of the writer's craft behind a knowing grin nearly 350 years ago: Writing, he said, is like prostitution. First you do it for love. Then you do it for a few friends. Finally you do it for money.

Molière had it mostly right, but there is a divergence between the trades. Not all prostitutes are volunteers, as all storytellers (with the possible exception of Scheherazade) have been and remain. Nobody asks us to do this, so the whining that stirred Wilson's bile is just about as he discerned it: not becoming. And, if we are to believe abundant lurid writings, inexperience is not always a handicap when it comes to hooking—indeed, it can be a positive marketing factor (moguls, sheiks: guys like that, it's said, really go for virgins). In my experience, at least, that is never the case for the writers. Experience counts in this line of work; one does not become a professional in this generation of writers without first having served a protracted, often painful, almost always unpaid novitiate. Still Molière's analogy mostly holds: until you get a few dents in you, the chances that you will write a story that impinges on the marrow of the reader are not very good.

Therefore the first presumption is that the person acquiring this text passed some time ago from the stage of doing it for love to the stage of accommodating a few friends, and is now not only ready but determined to try doing it for money.

The second presumption is that the person reading this book learned by heart in the earlier stages of writerly development the basic rules of grammar and syntax, and acquired as well not only the ability to spell several thousand English words correctly, but also an unabridged dictionary offering the correct spellings of the many thousands more of which each of us remains uncertain, *and the habit of using it.* In some respects, Maxwell Perkins, dead these many years after he by herculean effort transformed Thomas Wolfe's undisciplined outpourings into actual novels, did a pernicious disservice to writers of today; people who have never heard of Perkins or his patience with young Scribner's writers somehow imbibe the notion that all they need to do is get something on paper, and some editor somewhere, most likely with green eyeshade, will toil upon the bolus until it is fit for print. They are mistaken. There is only one way to sell your writing if you don't know how to write: that is to become so famous— or even better, so infamous—in another field that a packager of "books" masquerading as a publisher will hire some ink-stained wretch to turn it into English. If you harbor this notion, rid yourself of it; if you have not been arrested for doing something colorful, made the cover of *Time,* or huge amounts of money, all you have is your charm, and that will not be enough to catapult your grubby manuscript to the point of publication.

The third presumption is that there is a distinct possibility that you don't actually know how to read, and therefore operate under severe handicap when you proceed to write. This is not the insult that it may seem to be, and it is not the same thing as alleging that you are illiterate. It is simply a shorthand description of a condition that is extremely prevalent among perfectly intelligent adult Americans born since 1960, affecting also a fair number of those born before that arbitrarily designated date. Those who now find themselves unable to operate their VCRs or home computers with successful ease may vengefully blame their disability upon technological advances: "It's because of television." The more traditionally minded may wish to advert to the classical mode, ratifying Sigmund Freud's proposal that one's parents be held to account for all of one's shortcomings.

It doesn't matter which explanation is correct. Either way, the majority of American children entering the world since the fifties ended seem not to possess what for want of a better term may be called *a feel for the language*. When some of those former children, now independent adults, find their way into journalism and creative writing, they commonly display utter ignorance of the cadence and the rhythm of the American language, so that all of the richness that it delivers off the tongue—their tongues as much as anyone else's—vanishes in their translation of it to the written word. The sensory aspect of the language disappears in their transcriptions of it because their instruction in it never called that aspect to their attention.

Fortunately, this condition is curable, at any stage in life. All that is necessary is to do for yourself what was not done for you by your parents or other family members when you were young, either because you were watching television and could not be disturbed, or because they were watching television and did not wish to be: read good prose aloud. It is nice to possess a photographic recall of Aristotle's *Rhetoric* and his *Poetics*, and satisfying to rattle others' cages at cocktail parties by bombarding them with arcane terms for devices you recognize, but it is not necessary to acquire such erudition in order to write solid English prose effectively.

You can get what you need to write (as opposed to what you need to make a big nuisance of yourself at cocktail parties) by shutting yourself in a room by yourself for twenty minutes a day and reading aloud from E. B. White's *Charlotte's Web*, and going on from that to other works of skill, until you begin to see, *by hearing,* how much the choice and the arrangement of the words contribute to the impact of the story, even when no sound is uttered in its reading. And you will begin to see, very quickly—guaranteed. You will get the hang of it so fast that pretty soon you will be able to read aloud without making a sound, and you will enjoy it so much that you will discard with no regret, or even a backward glance, the arid and arduous approach that you took to books before. You will find, to your delight, that reading your own work aloud, even silently, is the most astonishingly easy and reliable method that there is for achieving economy in prose, efficiency of description, and narrative effect as well. Yes, there is a drawback: once you have picked up this technique, favored by professional writers who take pride in their work, you will reflexively identify the bad writing so often published by editors who despair of finding enough of the good stuff, and must settle for what they can get. Rely upon it: if you can read it aloud to yourself without wincing, you have probably gotten it right, however Aristotle might have defined what you did.

Conformably to that presumption, this manual includes numerous selections by writers whose work I consider exemplary. When I lead my seminars in this regimen, each participant at least twice per semester delivers such a selection. I think that is probably a more profitable situation than can be arranged by the person who must work alone—reading aloud to a group, after all, is the best approximation we moderns can engineer to the situation in which Homer smote his bloomin' lyre, and minstrels sang in mead halls of the epic deeds of yore. The listeners at public readings get the kind of stimulation that provokes them into pointing out nuances that the reader never would have noticed, had it not been for the performance. Still, one does the best one can in this world, and if there isn't any company, well, do it for yourself. You will only feel silly at first.

The fourth assumption is that you are able to approach this enterprise in roughly the same frame of mind as that of a trainee in a course in plumbing, airplane engine maintenance, or steam fitting. It is neither intended as, nor suitable for, the elevation of your understanding of literature, the refinement of your perceptions of such matters as symbolism and imagery, or your grasp of the author's place in his or her cultural and social milieu. Those are not negligible considerations when it comes to a critical appreciation of American and English literature, but they have no pertinence to the writer's task of writing *now;* they are matters for the reader, and so not on this agenda. Any improvement you may notice in your scholarly understanding will therefore be purely fortuitous. This is not about the *implications* of what Hemingway did, unintentionally or not; it is about *what* Hemingway did, and how to profit from it, and that is all.

2

If your reading hasn't made you a better person, and it hasn't, why the hell should your writing make your reader better?

It is always a comfort, no matter what one's project, to begin with a clear idea of the product desired from its completion. There is no substitute for knowing what you're doing. So, while most storytellers begin with no clear notion of how the story will turn out (that would take all the fun out of writing it), the assumption here is that you have in mind a work of fiction that will be readily and correctly received by the reader as a worthy addition to the stock of contemporary fiction written in English.

The first emphasis is on the adjective: *contemporary.* Prescind for the moment from the argumentative issue of whether what you like most to read—and therefore, most likely, aspire to imitate by writing—is properly labeled "modern" or "postmodern," and leave for future rumination as well whether what you write will be hailed as a revolutionary departure from everything that went before. Regardless of whether you relish the prospect, every reader who encounters your prose, whether amateur (your friends and family) or professional (heartless editors if you're unlucky, brilliantly insightful editors if you are blessed), with the first sentence will automatically commence the process of categorizing it, subjectively determining—often if not usually quite erroneously—where it belongs in the stream of current writing (I learned this the hard way: my first published book was categorized as a "hard-boiled detective story"—it was not—and most of the others since have been critically rated by reference to the same ill-chosen scale, thus neatly deflecting the general reader—the reader I have in mind—while deceitfully luring the crime-story addict. This leaves many in the first group cruelly deprived of acquaintance with my genius, many in the second group feeling themselves meanly bilked, and me with much smaller royalty checks than I would prefer to receive).

This is nothing more than a manifestation of the same compulsive behavior into which God craftily seduced Adam, giving him dominion over the birds of the air and the beasts of the field only in exchange for Adam's eager acquiescence in the task of naming them. The first thing the reader tries to do with what you have written is decide what it most resembles among other work he or she has read (or maybe merely heard about). If by chance your manuscript lights on the desk of a reader who has never recovered from the initial rush he felt when reading J. D. Salinger, and what you have done approximates Salinger's achievement in "For Esmé, with Love and Squalor," and the situations and the characters you depict resonate at all with those that Salinger portrayed, then you are in luck.

Some kind of luck, at least. If it is the good kind, and that editor liked Salinger, your submission will be seized upon and you have only to wait a bit until you become very rich. If your luck is bad, and that reader hated Salinger, your manuscript will be hurled on to the next reader (if not at once mailed back to you) with the disparagement that you are imitating Salinger. In neither event, you note, will the reader/editor actually advert to the truth of the matter: that his or her personal taste has led to views so pronounced of Salinger's work that they prevent him or her from reading impartially anything remotely like it. *The New Yorker* has repeatedly declined to publish stories I have written because the editors correctly —and, I initially and innocently thought, flatteringly—perceived the debt I owe to John O'Hara's ghost. As best I have been able to ascertain, none of them has seen fit to address the issue I sought to raise by the submission: "Is this story good enough, on its own merits, to be published in *The New Yorker?*"

There is, obviously, nothing you can do about that sort of thing. Paradoxically, that may be good: it means that you need not do what is not feasible—master all of recent writing (that being, say, what has been published to respectful reception in America and England since 1918) in order to frame for yourself a rough approximation of what you hope to write. No matter which models you choose, you will still be playing Russian roulette when you send out your manuscripts.

Still, it is helpful to understand broadly how fiction has changed since Daniel Defoe published *Robinson Crusoe* in 1719, and thus acquired his lasting if arguable reputation as the maker of the first novel in the English language. It is useful because that information firmly establishes the general, primary purpose of all fiction published since.

Long works of fiction are called "novels" because, in Defoe's age, manuscripts weighty enough to require binding as books consisted of reports of scientific inquiries and experiments, observations about the solar system, theological disquisitions, and records of daring explorations and arduous expeditions to remote lands. Defoe at least passively invited public confusion about the nature of his book: he pilfered, without attribution, the data he needed for his account of the sailor and his faithful companion from the report by one Alexander Selkirk of his 1704–1709 adventures as an island castaway. The public, accustomed to taking all objects— "books"—of similar size and heft as at least putatively truthful accounts of actual observations, deeds, and events, quite understandably accepted *Crusoe* as a story of things that had actually happened. Only gradually—and quite incompletely, during Defoe's lifetime—did it dawn upon his readers that he had made the whole thing up, artfully posing as the man of scientific mind marooned on a barren island all alone until Friday popped up.

In some quarters this discovery was deemed grounds for Defoe's condemnation as a charlatan, but more broadminded folks noted that he appeared to have contemplated no sly fraud to be advanced by means of his fabrications (what Selkirk may have thought of this I cannot say) and settled for making a noun out of what they found the book to be: something "novel." And in it as well lay the promise of the attitude that persists to this day: the assumption that all fiction is disguised biography, either the author's or another's (as, of course, to one degree or another, it is, but we will get to that issue later).

There is some reason to suspect that Defoe may have been at least initially as uncomprehending of his epoch-making achievement as his first readers were, accomplishing it more by serendipitous inadvertence than by conscious design. He was a malcontent and troublemaker, even by the rambunctious standards of his day. On religious matters, he stood as a Dissenter from the established Church of England, and was sufficiently bold in his public utterances and topical tracts to be fined, jailed, and pilloried. He later branched out into espionage, but found that too confining and moved on to the composition of political pamphlets that occasioned his prosecution first for treason and then for libel. He was, in other words, at least aware of the Draconian laws that limited freedom of speech to two varieties: that exercised by those in power and that extolling them as fine fellows; but he seems to have been too disrespectful and incautious to heed them (England's Licensing Act, permitting publication only after official review and approval—we Americans would call it "prior restraint," and at least officially forbid it with our First Amendment—expired in 1695, but the new permissiveness came at a price: if the target of the penman's vitriol cared to do so, he could have the insolent chap not only ruined, but jailed). The craft of fiction appealed to Defoe because at least putatively it enabled him to mock his betters—and thus, in his estimation, to advance the causes of social justice and religious liberty—without risking his own purse and hide.

What was under way was a gradual conversion of a people and its storytellers from dependence upon the oral medium that tradition had established for the preservation and dissemination of tales, sagas, and epics, to reliance upon the visual medium. In a panorama visible only in retrospect—certainly Defoe and his contemporaries had no notion of what lay in store, any more than Jane Austen did when *Sense and Sensibility* was published in 1811, or Norman Mailer did when *The Naked and the Dead* appeared in 1948— storytelling was becoming more and more a visual medium, the recipient at one anonymous remove collecting the story from the teller.

That process is still in progress today, somewhat to the dismay of those of us who deal primarily in printed fiction, as the descendants of readers occasionally beguiled by movies away from magazines and books now rely primarily on television and the movies to satisfy their appetites for stories. The visual media, using pictures that move instead of words that do not, carry a greater sensory impact than the visual medium that delivers the story by means of black marks on the white page. The consumer takes delivery much more passively, the eyes and ears registering images, noises, and the infrequent spoken words, reintegrating them into a more or less coherent story more or less the same as that the directors, actors, and screen editors depicted. And that story in its turn is more or less the same as the one contained in the script furnished by the screenwriter(s)—usually it is less the same, which is why screenwriters in general, especially screenwriters seduced from printed storytelling by promises of big money but unprepared for the experience of seeing *their* work transmogrified thrice over into something quite different (and also, perforce, nowhere near as good) become noticeably grouchy.

Nevertheless, as the delivery systems change, the original standards of judgment linger. One of them is the habit of assessing fiction according to its effectiveness as a purveyor of improving moral, ethical, and intellectual messages. That dates back from Defoe's day. The second half of the eighteenth century was besotted with imitations, some admitted, some bold counterfeits, of "medieval," classical, and Renaissance stories. The tacit understanding was that the entertainment value, if any, was an allowable if incidental aspect of the reader's exercise. When Jonathan Swift published his *Gulliver's Travels* in 1726, he did so as dean of St. Patrick's (Anglican) in Dublin, with the propagandistic intention of reminding his readers, bemused by science, to keep their vision firmly fixed on human weaknesses and sin. When Dickens published *Oliver Twist* 112 years later, he dutifully tugged a forelock of ambient deism toward the issue of sin and redemption, belabored the corrupting atmosphere of the poorhouses, and continued the practice of exacting the reader's guilt as his price for the enthralling story that he told.

There is in that no implied permit for superior snickering.

Our own age is just as stridently didactic. Fashion in criticism of American fiction of the late twentieth century displays the same deplorable tendency to weigh the story by assaying its weight as a message of Right Thinking. The only difference is that now the emphasis is more secular—or, as Swift might prefer, more profane. Now it is whether the story seems to inculcate views that the critic finds appropriate on issues of racism, sexism, ageism, jingoism, or any other of a hundred tedious issues on which the reader is suspected not only of harboring but of cherishing deviationist views. I think this is a lot of hogwash.

I also think it is damaging to the writer's professional development. This is because the writer cannot afford distractions in the composition of the story. Either he is going to allow the characters to develop the plot, thus leading to the resolution that concludes the tale, or else he is going to dragoon them into service of the moral that he wishes to convey.

When Charles Dickens began writing *Bleak House* (it was first published in book form in 1853), he toiled not only under the handicap of striving to deliver a message (he was convinced that the courts of Chancery by their refusal to decide cases promptly created more injustice than the wrongs alleged in them) but of his extraneous obligations as editor of the monthly periodical *Household Words*—he needed copy to fill the magazine, and his subscribers expected him to compose much of it (Fred Kaplan's *Dickens: A Biography*, published in 1988, neatly describes in detail the staggering workload Dickens carried, and deserves careful attention by the Dickens reader wishing to understand why the Inimitable —as he liked to call himself, perhaps half in deprecation—so infuriatingly persisted in combining good stories with interminable sermons). The following passage is from the opening of *Bleak House,* and should be read—aloud, of course —with that in mind.

London. Michaelmas term lately over, and the Lord Chancellor sitting in Lincoln's Inn Hall. Implacable November weather. As much mud in the streets, as if the waters had but newly retired from the face of the earth, and it would not be wonderful to meet a Megalosaurus, forty feet long or so, waddling like an elephantine lizard up Holborn Hill. Smoke lowering down from chimney-pots, making a soft black drizzle with flakes of soot in it as big as full-grown snowflakes—gone into mourning, one might imagine, for the death of the sun. Dogs, undistinguishable in mire. Horses, scarcely better; splashed to their very blinkers. Foot passengers, jostling one another's umbrellas, in a general infection of ill temper, and losing their foot-hold at street-corners, where tens of thousands of other foot passengers have been slipping and sliding since the day broke (if this day ever broke), adding new deposits to the crust upon crust of mud, sticking at those points tenaciously to the pavement, and accumulating at compound interest.

Fog everywhere. Fog up the river, where it flows among green aits and meadows; fog down the river, where it rolls defiled among the tiers of shipping, and the waterside pollutions of a great (and dirty) city. Fog on the Essex Marshes, fog on the Kentish heights. Fog creeping into the cabooses of collier-brigs; fog lying out on the yards, and hovering in the rigging of great ships; fog drooping on the gunwales of barges and small boats. Fog in the eyes and throats of ancient Greenwich pensioners, wheezing by the firesides of their wards; fog in the stem and bowl of the afternoon pipe of the wrathful skipper, down in his close cabin; fog cruelly pinching the toes and fingers of his shivering little 'prentice boy on deck. Chance people on the bridges peeping over the parapets into a nether sky of fog, with fog all round them, as if they were up in a balloon, and hanging in the misty clouds.

Gas looming through the fog in divers places in the streets, much as the sun may, from the spongey fields, be seen to loom by husbandman and ploughboy. Most of the shops lighted two hours before their time—as the gas seems to know, for it has a haggard and unwilling look.

The raw afternoon is rawest, and the dense fog is densest, and the muddy streets are muddiest, near that leaden-headed old obstruction, appropriate ornament for the threshold of a leaden-headed old corporation: Temple Bar. And hard by Temple Bar, in Lincoln's Inn Hall, at the very heart of the fog, sits the Lord High Chancellor in his High Court of Chancery.

Never can there come fog too thick, never can there come mud and mire too deep, to assort with the groping and floundering condition which this High Court of Chancery, most pestilent of hoary sinners, holds, this day, in the sight of heaven and earth.

On such an afternoon, if ever, the Lord High Chancellor ought to be sitting here—as here he is—with a foggy glory round his head, softly fenced in with crimson cloth and curtains, addressed by a large advocate with great whiskers, a little voice, and an interminable brief, and outwardly directing his contemplation to the lantern in the roof, where he can see nothing but fog. On such an afternoon, some score of members of the High Court of Chancery bar ought to be—as here they are—mistily engaged in one of the ten thousand stages of an endless cause, tripping one another up on slippery precedents, groping knee-deep in technicalities, running their goat-hair and horsehair warded heads against walls of words and making a pretence of equity with serious faces, as players might. On such an afternoon, the various solicitors in the cause, some two or three of whom have inherited it from their fathers, who made a fortune by it, ought to be—as are they not?—ranged in a line, in a long matted well (but you might look in vain for Truth at the bottom of it), between the registrar's red table and the silk gowns, with bills, cross-bills, answers, rejoinders, injunctions, affidavits, issues, references to masters, masters' reports, mountains of costly nonsense, piled before them. Well may the court be dim, with wasting candles here and there; well may the fog hang heavy in it, as if it would never get out; well may the stained-glass windows lose their colour, and admit no light of day into the place; well may the uninitiated from the streets, who peep in through the glass panes in the door, be deterred from entrance by its owlish aspect, and by the drawl languidly echoing to the roof from the padded dais where the Lord High Chancellor looks into the lantern that has no light in it, and where the attendant wigs are all stuck in a fog-bank! This is the Court of Chancery; which has its decaying houses and its blighted lands in every shire; which has its worn-out lunatic in every madhouse, and its dead in every churchyard; which has its ruined suitor, with his slipshod heels and threadbare dress, borrowing and begging through the round of every man's acquaintance; which gives to monied might the means abundantly of wearing out the right; which so exhausts finances, patience, courage, hope; so over-throws the brain and breaks the heart; that there is not an hon-ourable man among its practitioners who would not give—who does not often give—the warning, "Suffer any wrong that can be done you, rather than come here!"

Who happen to be in the Lord Chancellor's court this murky afternoon besides the Lord Chancellor, the counsel in the cause, two or three counsel who are never in any cause, and the well of solicitors before mentioned? There is the registrar below the Judge, in wig and gown; and there are two or three maces, or petty-bags, or privy-purses, or whatever they may be, in legal court suits. These are all yawning; for no crumb of amusement ever falls from J A R N D Y C E   A N D   J A R N D Y C E (the cause in hand), which was squeezed dry years upon years ago. The short-hand writers, the reporters of the court, and the reporters of the newspapers, invariably decamp with the rest of the regu-lars when Jarndyce and Jarndyce comes on. Their places are a blank. Standing on a seat at the side of the hall, the better to peer into the curtained sanctuary, is a little mad old woman in a squeezed bonnet, who is always in court, from its sitting to its rising, and always expecting some incomprehensible judgement to be given in her favour. Some say she really is, or was, a party to a suit; but no one knows for certain, because no one cares. She carries some small litter in a reticule which she calls her documents; principally consisting of paper matches and dry lavender. A sallow prisoner has come up, in custody, for the half-dozenth time, to make a personal application "to purge himself of his contempt"; which, being a solitary surviving executor who has fallen into a state of conglomeration about accounts of which it is not pretended that he had ever any knowledge, he is not at all likely ever to do. In the meantime his prospects in life are ended. Another ruined suitor, who periodically appears from Shropshire, and breaks out into efforts to address the Chancellor at the close of the day's business, and who can by no means be made to understand that the Chancellor is legally ignorant of his existence after making it desolate for a quarter of a century, plants himself in a good place and keeps an eye on the Judge, ready to call out "My Lord!" in a voice of sonorous complaint, on the instant of his rising. A few lawyers' clerks and others who know this suitor by sight, linger, on the chance of his furnishing some fun, and enlivening the dismal weather a little.

Jarndyce and Jarndyce drones on. This scarecrow of a suit has, in course of time, become so complicated that no man alive knows what it means. The parties to it understand it least; but it has been observed that no two Chancery lawyers can talk about it for five minutes without coming to a total disagreement as to all the premises. Innumerable children have been born into the cause; innumerable young people have married into it; innumerable old people have died out of it. Scores of persons have deliriously found themselves made parties in Jarndyce and Jarndyce, without knowing how or why; whole families have inherited legendary hatreds with the suit. The little plaintiff or defendant, who was promised a new rocking-horse when Jarndyce and Jarndyce should be settled, has grown up, possessed himself of a real horse, and trotted away into the other world. Fair wards of court have faded into mothers and grandmothers; a long procession of Chancellors has come in and gone out; the legion of bills in the suit have been transformed into mere bills of mortality; there are not three Jarndyces left upon the earth perhaps, since old Tom Jarndyce in despair blew his brains out at a coffee-house in Chancery Lane; but Jarndyce and Jarndyce still drags its dreary length before the Court, perennially hopeless.

Jarndyce and Jarndyce has passed into a joke. That is the only good that has ever come of it. It has been death to many, but it is a joke in the profession. Every master in Chancery has had a reference out of it. Every Chancellor was "in it," for somebody or other, when he was counsel at the bar. Good things have been said about it by blue-nosed, bulbous-shoed old benchers, in select port-wine committee after dinner in hall. Articled clerks have been in the habit of fleshing their legal wit upon it. The last Lord Chancellor handled it neatly, when, correcting Mr. Blowers the eminent silk gown who said that such a thing might happen when the sky rained potatoes, he observed, "or when we get through Jarndyce and Jarndyce, Mr. Blowers"—a pleasantry that particularly tickled the maces, bags, and purses.

How many people out of the suit, Jarndyce and Jarndyce has stretched forth its unwholesome hand to spoil and corrupt, would be a very wide question. From the master, upon whose impaling files reams of dusty warrants in Jarndyce and Jarndyce have grimly writhed into many shapes; down to the copying-clerk in the Six Clerks' Office, who has copied his tens of thousands of Chancery-folio-pages under that eternal heading; no man's nature has been made the better by it. In trickery, evasion, procrastination, spoliation, botheration, under false pretences of all sorts, there are influences that can never come to good. The very solicitors' boys who have kept the wretched suitors at bay, by protesting time out of mind that Mr. Chizzle, Mizzle, or otherwise, was particularly engaged and had appointments until dinner, may have got an extra moral twist and shuffle into themselves out of Jarndyce and Jarndyce. The receiver in the cause has acquired a goodly sum of money by it, but has acquired too a distrust of his own mother, and a contempt of his own kind. Chizzle, Mizzle, and otherwise, have lapsed into a habit of vaguely promising themselves that they will look into that outstanding little matter, and see what can be done for Drizzle— who was not well used—when Jarndyce and Jarndyce shall be got out of the office. Shirking and sharking, in all their many varieties, have been sown broadcast by the ill-fated cause; and even those who have contemplated its history from the outermost circle of such evil, have been insensibly tempted into a loose way of letting bad things alone to take their own bad course, and a loose belief that if the world go wrong, it was, in some offhand manner, never meant to go right.

Thus, in the midst of the mud and at the heart of the fog, sits the Lord High Chancellor in his High Court of Chancery.

"Mr. Tangle," says the Lord High Chancellor, latterly something restless under the eloquence of that learned gentleman.

"Mlud," says Mr. Tangle. Mr. Tangle knows more of Jarndyce and Jarndyce than anybody. He is famous for it—supposed never to have read anything else since he left school.

"Have you nearly concluded your argument?"

"Mlud, no—variety of points—feel it my duty to submit— ludship," is the reply that slides out of Mr. Tangle.

"Several members of the bar are still to be heard, I believe?" says the Chancellor, with a slight smile.

Eighteen of Mr. Tangle's learned friends, each armed with a little summary of eighteen hundred sheets, bob up like eighteen hammers in a pianoforte, make eighteen bows, and drop into their eighteen places of obscurity.

"We will proceed with the hearing on Wednesday fortnight," says the Chancellor. For the question at issue is only a question of costs, a mere bud on the forest tree of the parent suit, and really will come to a settlement one of these days.

The Chancellor rises; the bar rises; the prisoner is brought forward in a hurry; the man from Shropshire cries, "My lord!" Maces, bags, and purses, indignantly proclaim silence, and frown at the man from Shropshire.

"In reference," proceeds the Chancellor, still on Jarndyce and Jarndyce, "to the young girl—"

"Begludship's pardon—boy," says Mr. Tangle prematurely.

"In reference," proceeds the Chancellor, with extra distinctness, "to the young girl and boy, the two young people,"

(Mr. Tangle crushed.)

"Whom I directed to be in attendance today, and who are now in my private room, I will see them and satisfy myself as to the expediency of making the order for their residing with their uncle."

Mr. Tangle on his legs again.

"Begludship's pardon—dead."

"With their," Chancellor looking through his double eyeglass at the papers on his desk, "grandfather."

"Begludship's pardon—victim of rash action—brains."

Suddenly a very little counsel with a terrific bass voice, arises, fully inflated, in the back settlements of the fog, and says, "Will your lordship allow me? I appear for him. He is a cousin, several times removed. I am not at the moment prepared to inform the Court in what exact remove he is a cousin; but he *is* a cousin."

Leaving this address (delivered like a sepulchral message) ringing in the rafters of the roof, the very little counsel drops, and the fog knows him no more. Everybody looks for him. Nobody can see him.

"I will speak with both the young people," says the Chancellor anew, "and satisfy myself on the subject of their residing with their cousin. I will mention the matter tomorrow morning when I take my seat."

The Chancellor is about to bow to the bar, when the prisoner is presented. Nothing can possibly come of the prisoner's conglomeration, but his being sent back to prison; which is soon done. The man from Shropshire ventures another remonstrative "My lord!" but the Chancellor, being aware of him, has dexterously vanished. Everybody else quickly vanishes too. A battery of blue bags is loaded with heavy charges of papers and carried off by clerks; the little mad old woman marches off with her documents; the empty court is locked up. If all the injustice it has committed, and all the misery it has caused, could only be locked up with it, and the whole burnt away in a great funeral pyre—why, so much the better for other parties than the parties in Jarndyce and Jarndyce!

What Dickens was about there—in addition to filling the magazine—was setting an atmosphere. In my estimation he seriously overdid it; *prolix* is the word that springs to mind (a useful lesson here, to be kept in mind when infuriated by the outrageous demands of some loutishly insensitive editor or literary agent: Dickens had neither, and served as his own officer in both capacities; of course Agent Dickens and Editor Dickens thought all of Writer Dickens's stuff splendid, and wished not to trim a word from it).

But that estimation, it should be kept in mind, is an assessment made from a vantage point nearly 140 years farther down fiction's time line. Today's editors and publishers are most comfortable with novels of between 80,000 and 125,000 words; my rough calculations put *Bleak House* at around 378,000 words. George Eliot (Mary Ann Evans) initially published *Middlemarch,* that ghastly flagship among her four immensely ponderous novels (the other three are *Adam Bede, The Mill on the Floss,* and *Silas Marner*) employed by generations of English teachers to torment their helpless students, in eight volumes, commencing in December 1871 —and well she might have, with 323,664 words to print. The last of the installments appeared in December 1872, so her readers had a solid year to plod through a story that today's students are expected to master as but one of several books included on a term's reading list. The adult Victorians who read *Middlemarch* of course had other obligations of family and occupation that most twentieth-century undergraduates lack, but they also had some advantages denied to modern students: familiarity with the reform movements then enlivening British politics and informing the plot, but now musty debates to us; the relative absence of competing entertainments, except those performed live on the stage (Dickens and his friends made a profitable sideline of performing paid-admission "private theatricals") or at home; and a vastly slower pace of communications—the Royal Mail set it—that not only afforded them the leisure but stimulated the appetite for discursive writing. Well-known authors of fiction could indulge themselves then as most modern authors cannot: they could assume quite correctly that they monopolized the leisure-time attention of their grateful readers.

There is only one way to get away with that now, and the openings diminish every year. It is a two-part procedure. First you must establish yourself as a "popular"—i.e., entertaining, and nothing wrong with that—writer of fiction unashamedly based upon events of worldwide interest and general if imperfect understanding (sex is also a topic of reliable general interest, and it does no harm at all to include it with the rest of the action—provided, of course, that there *is* some other, more important action; otherwise what you're writing is trash at the best, and mere pornography at worst). World conflicts are the most reliable settings, but civil wars will do. Then you must somehow bring your name—not what you have written, but your name—to the forefront of the consciousness of the majority of Americans who seldom read books.

This is another way of saying that if you are James Michener, and you write a *Tales of the South Pacific* setting *Romeo and Juliet* in the conflict that began at Pearl Harbor, you will probably do pretty well, but if that book becomes the basis of a hit Broadway musical called *South Pacific,* and that in turn becomes the basis for a movie, *South Pacific,* thereafter you can be as windy as you like. Or you might try to emulate Margaret Mitchell's success in romanticizing the American Civil War (*Gone With the Wind*), or Herman Wouk (*The Caine Mutiny*). Be careful, though, if you choose Mitchell for your model; she was killed in a highway accident before she could do a sequel. Be prudent as well if Thomas Heggen (*Mister Roberts*) seems worthy of emulation; he destroyed himself before he could capitalize on his success. It is essential that you follow today's version of the formula exactly: from book to stage, screen, or TV. Do not on any account get the crazy idea that you can gain a large audience for a big, fat novel, even a very fine one, by first establishing yourself in the public mind as a speechwriter in the Nixon administration, and then going on to become a widely respected columnist for *The New York Times:* William Safire tried that when he delivered (another rough guess) 625,000 words (plus another 132 pages of sources and commentary) under the title *Freedom: A Novel of Abraham Lincoln and the Civil War,* in 1987; it is a wonderful book, the tale of Lincoln that Gore Vidal would have written had he had the talent, but it went widely unread. Novels that retail for close to thirty bucks have a way of doing that.

That is because the only people who have time to read long novels today are people who make their livings, and therefore spend their working hours, reading novels. They do not buy those novels. Most of them—the ones who matter to you, at least—are the editors and publishers who read them, not for enjoyment (although the ones whom I know do enjoy them) but in order to decide whether they can make money for their companies by publishing them. If you are not known to them as someone who writes novels that sell like Dickens to people who do not ordinarily buy books, you are going to have to persuade them to publish your novel by writing one short enough to sell at a profit to the comparatively few habitual readers who buy novels that they understand to be good. And that means: between 80,000 and 125,000 words.

I think the best way to start to do this (assuming, of course, that you have stories to tell—patience, patience, we will get to that next) is to read, aloud, from the works of the writer who for all practical purposes formed the American style for this century. That was Ernest Hemingway. If you wish to know what a son of a bitch he could be (not that there aren't a lot of other good reasons to learn about him) read Jeffrey Meyers's lucid and dispassionate *Hemingway* (Harper & Row, 1985). If you wish to learn how to write, read Hemingway himself. What next follows is the best opening chapter I have ever read. It is from *A Farewell to Arms*.

In the late summer of that year we lived in a house in a village that looked across the river and the plain to the mountains. In the bed of the river there were pebbles and boulders, dry and white in the sun, and the water was clear and swiftly moving and blue in the channels. Troops went by the house and down the road and the dust they raised powdered the leaves of the trees. The trunks of the trees too were dusty and the leaves fell early that year and we saw the troops marching along the road and the dust rising and leaves, stirred by the breeze, falling and the soldiers marching and afterward the road bare and white except for the leaves.

The plain was rich with crops; there were many orchards of fruit trees and beyond the plain the mountains were brown and bare. There was fighting in the mountains and at night we could see the flashes from the artillery. In the dark it was like summer lightning, but the nights were cool and there was not the feeling of a storm coming.

Sometimes in the dark we heard the troops marching under the window and guns going past pulled by motor-tractors. There was much traffic at night and many mules on the roads with boxes of ammunition on each side of their pack-saddles and gray motor trucks that carried men, and other trucks with loads covered with canvas that moved slower in the traffic. There were big guns too that passed in the day drawn by tractors, the long barrels of the guns covered with green branches and green leafy branches and vines laid over the tractors. To the north we could look across a valley and see a forest of chestnut trees and behind it another mountain on this side of the river. There was fighting for that mountain too, but it was not successful, and in the fall when the rains came the leaves all fell from the chestnut trees and the branches were bare and the trunks black with rain. The vineyards were thin and bare-branched too and all the country was wet and brown and dead with autumn. There were mists over the river and clouds on the mountain and the trucks splashed mud on the road and the troops were muddy and wet in their capes; their rifles were wet and under their capes the two leather cartridge boxes on the front of the belts, gray leather boxes heavy with packs of clips of thin, long 6.5 mm. cartridges, bulged forward under the capes so that the men, passing on the road, marched as though they were six months gone with child.

There were small gray motor cars that passed going very fast; usually there was an officer on the seat with the driver and more officers in the back seat. They splashed more mud than the camions even and if one of the officers in the back was very small and he was sitting between two generals, he himself so small that you could not see his face but only the top of his cap and his narrow back, and the car went especially fast it was probably the King. He lived in Udine and came out this way nearly every day to see how things were going, and things went very badly.

At the start of the winter came the permanent rain and with

the rain came the cholera. But it was checked and in the end only seven thousand died of it in the army.

If you compare the 608 words that Hemingway used to set the stage for his story about World War I in Italy with the 2,800 or so that Dickens devoted to creating the ambience for the story of a lawsuit, you will, I think, be hard-pressed to say that Hemingway's approach suffers by comparison (although I for one would punctuate it somewhat more generously— and that sort of *lèse majesté* attitude is another serviceable habit for the developing writer to acquire: the masters whose work has justifiably stood up for decades, and rings as true today as the day when it was printed, are not for that reason to be taken as perfect. It is necessary, while learning from them, not to be intimidated, and to remember they didn't tell all of the stories, or invariably tell the ones they picked with ultimate, unapproachable skill). Of course it could be argued pretty convincingly that Hemingway's service as an ambulance driver in a war did not cultivate in him the leisurely manner Dickens acquired from his experience as a court reporter, but the practical fact remains: writers hoping to sell their fiction in the last quarter of the twentieth century are best advised to prefer the plain style, and when possible to use 608 words instead of 2,800, no matter what the story. Hemingway, after all, in 1929 had only the automobile, the train, the streetcar, the movies, the gramophone, and radio to keep his potential readers too occupied to read him. Your competition, especially television, is stronger, far wealthier, more insistent, and omnipresent, and the people in positions to buy work from you are acutely aware of it—it competes for their time, too.

3

First: Know thyself
  –Plutarch
Then: Try to keep it to yourself
  –Higgins

The inscription Plutarch found at the Oracle of Delphi is good instruction for the person who would become a responsible adult, a state to which even writers can aspire without denying their ambitions. The difficulties begin when as postulants hoping to become novices we youthfully confide those ambitions to adults whom we think trustworthy and more savvy in such matters than we. Because most of us in America are still in school when the Muse first bites (or seek attention to the wound by returning to school for diagnosis), these adults are usually teachers.

This is as it should be. Good teachers, after all, have much to answer for when it comes to assigning responsibility for the inflammation that itches young people to become writers. They are the ones who communicate the rash by recklessly inciting young passions for prose, and it is only to be expected that some of their charges will develop cases so virulent that they can only be temporarily palliated—but never cured; there is no cure—by writing. And then only endured, over a lifetime of certain affliction, by seeing what we've written in print. Invariably these good people, our mentors and trusted friends, cruelly tell us: "Write about what you know."

This is because they wish to be tactful and don't know what else to say. "Oh, you poor bastard" would be a kinder answer—though less sympathetic, more honest—but even saintly Father Damien in his capacity as host of the leper colony on Molokai would have shrunk from such candor with his charges. The cruelty is not in the objective validity of the advice—if you are writing about something that you *don't* know, after all, virtually any reader above the age of reason will perceive your fatuity at once—but in the implication that what the beginner knows is something that will interest a third-party stranger.

That is almost never the case, because what the young writer knows, and finds most fascinating, is the young person the young writer is. The decade between twelve and twenty-two is the pool of Narcissus for most people. The process of first getting ready to become an adult (the year or so when the glands first kick in, and the hormones start raging through the bloodstream), and then becoming one, is endlessly fascinating to experience. Therefore it occupies much if not most of the self-observer's attention, and is consequently most assuredly what he or she knows best—and you don't have to go to the library in the rain to study it, because it's right there in your pants.

The trouble is that while the process is by turns exhilarating and depressing to experience, and quite understandably absorbing to the subject, *everybody who is older already knows about it.* Well, maybe not everybody; some people manage to live a great many years, a few their entire lives, without ever catching the drift of matters, but very few of them secure employment as editors and publishers, and the majority of the more normal, who do obtain such jobs, find first-hand reports of such adolescent excitements utterly boring.

All writing that intrigues intelligent readers—the people you are presumably after—is news. They read papers and books to acquire information that they did not have before. What we call "news"—truthful reports, whether published in print or by broadcast, of facts about people and interesting events of major or minor importance—consists of presumably unembellished observations kindly provided by someone who had the good or evil fortune to be present at the scene where the people either caused the event, or the event happened to the people. In other words, it is gossip, but *important, verified,* gossip. It is also uncensored: the reporter obedient to the rules is restricted to snide innuendo when it comes to suggesting the actual—if nefarious—motives and probable veracity of the parties to the occurrence.

Good fiction is *un*verified, uncensored gossip. The person who writes it does so under no obligation other than that of making it seem to have taken place. The story must seem to be true, which is another way of saying that it must be gossip of such quality that the reader is seduced into invocation of a self-deceiving attitude: This story is so good that if it isn't true, it should be.

This is called "the willing suspension of disbelief," precisely the act that the coy seducee commits when the silver-tongued seducer obtains the cooperation desired—by both—by means of a firm promise of respect in the morning. But the person who is writing the story, perhaps paradoxically enough, ought to be even more circumspect when dealing with the characters engaged in its performance.

This is because the writer of fiction gets to rig the occasion.

The reporter of fact is not supposed to do that, and usually can't. The reason that the media pounce on public figures—whom the reporters have long known to be sanctimonious frauds—when they get into scrapes and then try to lie about it, is that the reporters have yearned for the chance to unmask them for the hypocrites they are, and have finally been vouchsafed permission. What makes the occasion especially delicious is that the fraud has foolishly issued the permit himself.

Only stupid people gossip about themselves. Those who tell tales, true or false, about how wonderful they are (as demonstrated by their marvelous accomplishments) are called "braggarts." Those who recount how miserable they are (as demonstrated by the resolute refusal of the whole world to understand how special they are, and accordingly be especially nice to them) are called "jerks." Those who stand back from the braggarts and jerks, and take supercilious note of their stupid behavior, are called "prigs." Each of these terms has many synonyms, all them generally apropos, some of them obscene.

Stupid people do not write good fiction. Arrogant, smart people write good fiction. Their arrogance is what impels them to demand center stage as the tellers of the stories. Their intelligence is what enables them to conceal that arrogance. If you are a good writer, you are a sneak. Much of what you write will indeed be about what you know, and much of that in turn will be about what you have learned of yourself, warts and all. But while most will suspect this, and many will allege it, none will ever be sure. They will not be sure even if you tell them their suspicions are correct, and if you insist they are correct, they will know that you are lying.

Thomas Wolfe was an extremely stupid person, and no sneak at all. He wrote very bad books. It is a wonder to me that Maxwell Perkins, no slouch at sneakiness himself, could stand him, and a source of absolute astonishment that anyone read, let alone purchased, his interminable novels. I have *Look Homeward, Angel* and *Of Time and the River* in my own library. I bought those books with my own money when I was in college, and I read them before I was twenty, and I was enthralled. I was enthralled because I was reading Thomas Wolfe at the proper time in my life. If you have not read the Jack Kerouac of the Twenties before you turn twenty, don't (if you are not yet thirty, and reading Henry James of your own volition, cut it out; you're not ready).

Wolfe knew but one thing: that he was unique, and that no male in the history of the world had ever been so puissant, intelligent, tormented, abused, misunderstood, horny, and thirsty as he (if you want more proof than his novels furnish of the truth of those allegations—God only knows why you would—consult Elizabeth Nowell's fine biography, *Thomas Wolfe*). He was as old as the century when he died in 1938— Perkins spliced up *The Web and the Rock* (published in 1939, ten years after *Angel*) and *You Can't Go Home Again* (1940) from stuff cut from the first two tomes—but he was writing for the Victorian era he had missed. He was not smart enough to stay out of his stories.

Then again (and more likely): perhaps he didn't have any stories to tell, except those about himself. Wolfe did only three things in his life. He grew up in Asheville, North Carolina. He went to school: first the University of North Carolina, graduating in 1920, then Harvard, earning his master's in 1922. He taught English at New York University until 1930, a year after *Angel* loosed him upon an unsuspecting populace and confirmed his manifest belief that no one with the possible exception of Jesus had ever been the man he was. Those were the only data he had: the ones he acquired by first wishing to be, and then becoming, A Writer. He had no stories to tell, except those of himself.

I do not choose to inflict upon you here a selection from Thomas Wolfe's work. He was a writer who never got beyond the first phase described by Molière. As long as Wolfe lived, which was not very long, he did it for love, and it was self-love. Only good luck got him money for doing it. If you are over twenty, and you have escaped him, thank your lucky stars. His work is significant for anyone wishing to understand American literature of the twentieth century, but it is poison for anyone bent upon contributing to that literature. There are much better masters.

One of them is Gay Talese. Talese went to work for *The New York Times* in 1956, after the University of Alabama and two years of military service, and remained there into 1965. In the meantime, beginning in 1960, he moonlighted as a free-lancer for *Esquire* magazine, for which he did some stuff (collected as *Fame and Obscurity* and published in 1970) that was absolutely crystalline. My favorite among the pieces in that work is "The Silent Season of a Hero," first published in 1966. It is about Joe DiMaggio.

> "I would like to take the great DiMaggio fishing," the old man said. "They say his father was a fisherman. Maybe he was as poor as we are and would understand."
>
> –Ernest Hemingway, *The Old Man and the Sea*

It was not quite spring, the silent season before the search for salmon, and the old fishermen of San Francisco were either painting their boats or repairing their nets along the pier or sitting in the sun talking quietly among themselves, watching the tourists come and go, and smiling, now, as a pretty girl paused to take their picture. She was about twenty-five, healthy and blue-eyed and wearing a red turtle-neck sweater, and she had long, flowing blonde hair that she brushed back a few times before clicking her camera. The fishermen, looking at her, made admiring comments but she did not understand because they spoke a Sicilian dialect; nor did she notice the tall grey-haired man in a dark suit who stood watching her from behind a big bay window on the second floor of DiMaggio's Restaurant that overlooks the pier.

He watched until she left, lost in the crowd of newly arrived tourists that had just come down the hill by cable car. Then he sat down again at the table in the restaurant, finishing his tea and lighting another cigarette, his fifth in the last half hour. It was eleven-thirty in the morning. None of the other tables was occupied, and the only sounds came from the bar where a liquor salesman was laughing at something the headwaiter had said. But then the salesman, his briefcase under his arm, headed for the door, stopping briefly to peek into the dining room and call out, "See you later, Joe." Joe DiMaggio turned and waved at the salesman. Then the room was quiet again.

At fifty-one, DiMaggio was a most distinguished-looking man, aging as gracefully as he had played on the ball field, impeccable in his tailoring, his nails manicured, his six-foot two-inch body seeming as lean and capable as when he posed for the portrait that hangs in the restaurant and shows him in Yankee Stadium swinging from the heels at a pitch thrown twenty years ago. His grey hair was thinning at the crown, but just barely, and his face was lined in the right places, and his expression, once as sad and haunted as a matador's, was more in repose these days, though, as now, tension had returned and he chain-smoked and occasionally paced the floor and looked out the window at the people below. In the crowd was a man he did not wish to see.

The man had met DiMaggio in New York. This week he had come to San Francisco and had telephoned several times but none of the calls had been returned because DiMaggio suspected that the man, who had said he was doing research on some vague sociological project, really wanted to delve into DiMaggio's private life and that of DiMaggio's former wife, Marilyn Monroe. DiMaggio would never tolerate this. The memory of her death is still very painful to him, and yet, because he keeps it to himself, some people are not sensitive to it. One night in a supper club a woman who had been drinking approached his table, and when he did not ask her to join him, she snapped:

"All right, I guess I'm *not* Marilyn Monroe."

He ignored her remark, but when she repeated it, he replied, barely controlling his anger, "No—I wish you were, but you're not."

The tone of his voice softened her, and she asked, "Am I saying something wrong?"

"You already have," he said. "Now will you please leave me alone?"

His friends on the wharf, understanding him as they do, are very careful when discussing him with strangers, knowing that should they inadvertently betray a confidence he will not denounce them but rather will never speak to them again; this comes from a sense of propriety not inconsistent in the man who also, after Marilyn Monroe's death, directed that fresh flowers be placed on her grave "forever."

Some of the older fishermen who have known DiMaggio all his life remember him as a small boy who helped clean his father's boat, and as a young man who sneaked away and used a broken oar as a bat on the sandlots nearby. His father, a small mustachioed man known as Zio Pepe, would become infuriated and call him *lagnuso*, lazy, *meschino*, good-for-nothing, but in 1936 Zio Pepe was among those who cheered when Joe DiMaggio returned to San Francisco after his first season with the New York Yankees and was carried along the wharf on the shoulders of the fishermen.

The fishermen also remember how, after his retirement in 1951, DiMaggio brought his second wife, Marilyn, to live near the wharf, and sometimes they would be seen early in the morning fishing off DiMaggio's boat, the *Yankee Clipper*, now docked quietly in the marina, and in the evening they would be sitting and talking on the pier. They had arguments, too, the fishermen knew, and one night Marilyn was seen running hysterically, crying as she ran, along the road away from the pier, with Joe following. But the fishermen pretended they did not see this; it was none of their affair. They knew that Joe wanted her to stay in San Francisco and avoid the sharks in Hollywood, but she was confused and torn then—"She was a child," they said—and even today DiMaggio loathes Los Angeles and many of the people in it. He no longer speaks to his onetime friend, Frank Sinatra, who had befriended Marilyn in her final years, and he also is cool to Dean Martin and Peter Lawford and Lawford's former wife, Pat, who once gave a party at which she introduced Marilyn Monroe to Robert Kennedy, and the two of them danced often that night, Joe heard, and he did not take it well. He was very possessive of her that year, his close friends say, because Marilyn and he had planned to remarry; but before they could she was dead, and DiMaggio banned the Lawfords and Sinatra and many Hollywood people from her funeral. When Marilyn Monroe's attorney complained that DiMaggio was keeping her friends away, DiMaggio answered coldly, "If it weren't for those friends persuading her to stay in Hollywood she would still be alive."

Joe DiMaggio now spends most of the year in San Francisco, and each day tourists, noticing the name on the restaurant, ask the men on the wharf if they ever see him. Oh yes, the men say, they see him nearly every day; they have not seen him yet this morning, they add, but he should be arriving shortly. So the tourists continue to walk along the piers past the crab vendors, under the circling sea gulls, past the fish 'n' chip stands, sometimes stopping to watch a large vessel steaming toward the Golden Gate Bridge which, to their dismay, is painted red. Then they visit the Wax Museum, where there is a life-size figure of DiMaggio in uniform, and walk across the street and spend a quarter to peer through the silver telescopes focused on the island of Alcatraz, which is no longer a Federal prison. Then they return to ask the men if DiMaggio has been seen. Not yet, the men say, although they notice his blue Impala parked in the lot next to the restaurant. Sometimes tourists will walk into the restaurant and have lunch and will see him sitting calmly in a corner signing autographs and being extremely gracious with everyone. At other times, as on this particular morning when the man from New York chose to visit, DiMaggio was tense and suspicious.

When the man entered the restaurant from the side steps leading to the dining room he saw DiMaggio standing near the window talking with an elderly maître d' named Charles Friscia. Not wanting to walk in and risk intrusion, the man asked one of DiMaggio's nephews to inform Joe of his presence. When DiMaggio got the message he quickly turned and left Friscia and disappeared through an exit leading down to the kitchen.

Astonished and confused, the visitor stood in the hall. A moment later Friscia appeared and the man asked, "Did Joe leave?"

"Joe who?" Friscia replied.

"Joe DiMaggio!"

"Haven't seen him," Friscia said.

"You haven't *seen* him! He was standing right next to you a second ago!"

"It wasn't me," Friscia said.

"You were standing next to him. I saw you. In the dining room."

"You must be mistaken," Friscia said, softly, seriously. "It wasn't me."

"You *must* be kidding," the man said, angrily, turning and leaving the restaurant. Before he could get to his car, however, DiMaggio's nephew came running after him and said, "Joe wants to see you."

He returned expecting to see DiMaggio waiting for him. Instead he was handed a telephone. The voice was powerful and deep and so tense that the quick sentences ran together.

"You are invading my rights, I did not ask you to come, I assume you have a lawyer, you must have a lawyer, get your lawyer!"

"I came as a friend," the man interrupted.

"That's beside the point," DiMaggio said. "I have my privacy, I do not want it violated, you'd better get a lawyer. . . ." Then, pausing, DiMaggio asked, "Is my nephew there?"

He was not.

"Then wait where you are."

A moment later DiMaggio appeared, tall and red-faced, erect and beautifully dressed in his dark suit and white shirt with the grey silk tie and the gleaming silver cuff links. He moved with big steps toward the man and handed him an airmail envelope, unopened, that the man had written from New York.

"Here," DiMaggio said. "This is yours."

Then DiMaggio sat down at a small table. He said nothing, just lit a cigarette and waited, legs crossed, his head held high and back so as to reveal the intricate construction of his nose, a fine sharp tip above the big nostrils and tiny bones built out from the bridge, a great nose.

"Look," DiMaggio said, more calmly. "I do not interfere with other people's lives. And I do not expect them to interfere with mine. There are things about my life, personal things, that I refuse to talk about. And even if you asked my brothers they would be unable to tell you about them because they do not know. There are things about me, so many things, that they simply do not know. . . ."

"I don't want to cause trouble," the man said. "I think you're a great man, and. . . ."

"I'm not great," DiMaggio cut in. "I'm not great," he repeated, softly. "I'm just a man trying to get along."

Then DiMaggio, as if realizing that he was intruding upon his own privacy, abruptly stood up. He looked at his watch.

"I'm late," he said, very formal again. "I'm ten minutes late. *You're* making me late."

The man left the restaurant. He crossed the street and wandered over to the pier, briefly watching the fishermen hauling their nets and talking in the sun, seeming very calm and contented. Then, after he had turned and was headed back toward the parking lot, a blue Impala stopped in front of him and Joe DiMaggio leaned out the window and asked, "Do you have a car?" His voice was very gentle.

"Yes," the man said.

"Oh," DiMaggio said. "I would have given you a ride."

JOE DiMAGGIO was not born in San Francisco but in Martinez, a small fishing village twenty-five miles northeast of the Golden Gate. Zio Pepe had settled there after leaving Isola delle Femmine, an islet off Palermo where the DiMaggios had been fishermen for generations. But in 1915, hearing of the luckier waters off San Francisco's wharf, Zio Pepe left Martinez, packing his boat with furniture and family, including Joe who was one year old.

San Francisco was placid and picturesque when the DiMaggios arrived, but there was a competitive undercurrent and struggle for power along the pier. At dawn the boats would sail out to where the bay meets the ocean and the sea is rough, and later the men would race back with their hauls, hoping to beat their fellow fishermen to shore and sell it while they could. Twenty or thirty boats would sometimes be trying to gain the channel shoreward at the same time, and a fisherman had to know every rock in the water, and later know every bargaining trick along the shore, because the dealers and restaurateurs would play one fisherman off against the other, keeping the prices down. Later the fishermen became wiser and organized, predetermining the maximum amount each fisherman would catch, but there were always some men who, like the fish, never learned, and so heads would sometimes be broken, nets slashed, gasoline poured onto their fish, flowers of warning placed outside their doors.

But these days were ending when Zio Pepe arrived, and he expected his five sons to succeed him as fishermen, and the first two, Tom and Michael, did; but a third, Vincent, wanted to sing. He sang with such magnificent power as a young man that he came to the attention of the great banker, A. P. Giannini, and there were plans to send him to Italy for tutoring and the opera. But there was hesitation around the DiMaggio household and Vince never went; instead he played ball with the San Francisco Seals and sportswriters misspelled his name.

It was DeMaggio until Joe, at Vince's recommendation, joined the team and became a sensation, being followed later by the youngest brother, Dominic, who was also outstanding. All three later played in the big leagues and some writers like to say that Joe was the best hitter, Dom the best fielder, Vince the best singer, and Casey Stengel once said: "Vince is the only player I ever saw who could strike out three times in one game and not be embarrassed. He'd walk into the clubhouse whistling. Everybody would be feeling sorry for him, but Vince always thought he was doing good."

After he retired from baseball Vince became a bartender, then a milkman, now a carpenter. He lives forty miles north of San Francisco in a house he partly built, has been happily married for thirty-four years, has four grandchildren, has in the closet one of Joe's tailor-made suits that he has never had altered to fit, and when people ask if he envies Joe he always says, "No, maybe Joe would like to have what I have. He won't admit it, but he just might like to have what I have." The brother Vince most admired was Michael, "a big earthy man, a dreamer, a fisherman who wanted things but didn't want to take from Joe, or to work in the restaurant. He wanted a bigger boat, but wanted to earn it on his own. He never got it." In 1953, at the age of forty-four, Michael fell from his boat and drowned.

Since Zio Pepe's death at seventy-seven in 1949, Tom, at sixty-two the oldest brother—two of his four sisters are older—has become nominal head of the family and manages the restaurant that was opened in 1937 as Joe DiMaggio's Grotto. Later Joe sold out his share and now Tom is the co-owner of it with Dominic. Of all the brothers, Dominic, who was known as the "Little Professor" when he played with the Boston Red Sox, is the most successful in business. He lives in a fashionable Boston suburb with his wife and three children and is president of a firm that manufactures fiber-cushion materials and grossed more than $3,500,000 last year.

Joe DiMaggio lives with his widowed sister, Marie, in a tan stone house on a quiet residential street not far from Fisherman's Wharf. He bought the house almost thirty years ago for his parents, and after their death he lived there with Marilyn Monroe; now it is cared for by Marie, a slim and handsome dark-eyed woman who has an apartment on the second floor, Joe on the third. There are some baseball trophies and plaques in the small room off DiMaggio's bedroom, and on his dresser are photographs of Marilyn Monroe, and in the living room downstairs is a small painting of her that DiMaggio likes very much: it reveals only her face and shoulders and she is wearing a very wide-brimmed sun hat, and there is a soft sweet smile on her lips, an innocent curiosity about her that is the way he saw her and the way he wanted her to be seen by others—a simple girl, "a warm bighearted girl," he once described her, "that everybody took advantage of."

The publicity photographs emphasizing her sex appeal often offended him, and a memorable moment for Billy Wilder, who directed her in *The Seven Year Itch,* occurred when he spotted DiMaggio in a large crowd of people gathered on Lexington Avenue in New York to watch a scene in which Marilyn, standing over a subway grating to cool herself, had her skirts blown high by a sudden wind below. "What the hell is going on here?" DiMaggio was overheard to have said in the crowd, and Wilder recalled, "I shall never forget the look of death on Joe's face."

He was then thirty-nine, she was twenty-seven. They had been married in January of that year, 1954, despite disharmony in temperament and time: he was tired of publicity, she was thriving on it; he was intolerant of tardiness, she was always late. During their honeymoon in Tokyo an American general had in-

troduced himself and asked if, as a patriotic gesture, she would
visit the troops in Korea. She looked at Joe. "It's your honeymoon," he said, shrugging, "go ahead if you want to."

She appeared on ten occasions before 100,000 servicemen,
and when she returned she said, "It was so wonderful, Joe. You
never heard such cheering."

"Yes I have," he said.

ACROSS FROM HER PORTRAIT in the living room, on a coffee table
in front of a sofa, is a sterling-silver humidor that was presented
to him by his Yankee teammates at a time when he was the most
talked-about man in America, and when Les Brown's band had
recorded a hit that was heard day and night on the radio:

> . . . From Coast to Coast, that's all you hear
> Of Joe the One-Man Show
> He's glorified the horsehide sphere,
> Jolting Joe DiMaggio . . .
> Joe . . . Joe . . . DiMaggio . . . we
> want you on our side. . . .

The year was 1941, and it began for DiMaggio in the middle of
May after the Yankees had lost four games in a row, seven of
their last nine, and were in fourth place, five-and-a-half games
behind the leading Cleveland Indians. On May 15th, DiMaggio
hit only a first-inning single in a game that New York lost to Chicago, 13–1; he was barely hitting .300, and had greatly disappointed the crowds that had seen him finish with a .352 average
the year before and .381 in 1939.

He got a hit in the next game, and the next, and the next. On
May 24th, with the Yankees losing 6–5 to Boston, DiMaggio
came up with runners on second and third and singled them
home, winning the game, extending his streak to ten games. But
it went largely unnoticed. Even DiMaggio was not conscious of it

until it had reached twenty-nine games in mid-June. Then the newspapers began to dramatize it, the public became aroused, they sent him good-luck charms of every description, and DiMaggio kept hitting, and radio announcers would interrupt programs to announce the news, and then the song again: *"Joe . . . Joe . . . DiMaggio . . . we want you on our side. . . ."*

Sometimes DiMaggio would be hitless his first three times up, the tension would build, it would appear that the game would end without his getting another chance—but he always would, and then he would hit the ball against the left-field wall, or through the pitcher's legs, or between two leaping infielders. In the forty-first game, the first of a double-header in Washington, DiMaggio tied an American League record that George Sisler had set in 1922. But before the second game began a spectator sneaked onto the field and into the Yankees' dugout and stole DiMaggio's favorite bat. In the second game, using another of his bats, DiMaggio lined out twice and flied out. But in the seventh inning, borrowing one of his old bats that a teammate was using, he singled and broke Sisler's record, and he was only three games away from surpassing the major-league record of forty-four set in 1897 by Willie Keeler while playing for Baltimore when it was a National League franchise.

An appeal for the missing bat was made through the newspapers. A man from Newark admitted the crime and returned it with regrets. And on July 2, at Yankee Stadium, DiMaggio hit a home run into the left-field stands. The record was broken.

He also got hits in the next eleven games, but on July 17th in Cleveland, at a night game attended by 67,468, he failed against two pitchers, Al Smith and Jim Bagby, Jr., although Cleveland's hero was really its third baseman, Ken Keltner, who in the first inning lunged to his right to make a spectacular backhanded stop of a drive and, from the foul line behind third base, he threw DiMaggio out. DiMaggio received a walk in the fourth inning. But in the seventh he again hit a hard shot at Keltner, who again stopped it and threw him out. DiMaggio hit sharply toward the shortstop in the eighth inning, the ball taking a bad hop; but Lou Boudreau speared it off his shoulder and threw to the second baseman to start a double play and DiMaggio's streak was stopped at fifty-six games. But the New York Yankees were on their way to winning the pennant by seventeen games, and the World Series too, and so in August, in a hotel suite in Washington, the players threw a surprise party for DiMaggio and toasted him with champagne and presented him with this Tiffany silver humidor that is now in San Francisco in his living room. . . .

MARIE WAS IN THE KITCHEN making toast and tea when DiMaggio came down for breakfast; his grey hair was uncombed but, since he wears it short, it was not untidy. He said good-morning to Marie, sat down and yawned. He lit a cigarette. He wore a blue wool bathrobe over his pajamas. It was eight a.m. He had many things to do today and he seemed cheerful. He had a conference with the president of Continental Television, Inc., a large retail chain in California of which he is a partner and vice-president; later he had a golf date, and then a big banquet to attend, and, if that did not go on too long and he were not too tired afterward, he might have a date.

Picking up the morning paper, not rushing to the sports page, DiMaggio read the front-page news, the people-problems of '66: Kwame Nkrumah was overthrown in Ghana, students were burning their draft cards (DiMaggio shook his head), the flu epidemic was spreading through the whole state of California. Then he flipped inside through the gossip columns, thankful they did not have him in there today—they had printed an item about his dating "an electrifying airline hostess" not long ago, and they also spotted him at dinner with Dori Lane, "the frantic frugger" in Whiskey à Go Go's glass cage—and then he turned to the sports page and read a story about how the injured Mickey Mantle may never regain his form.

It had all happened so quickly, the passing of Mantle, or so it seemed; he had succeeded DiMaggio as DiMaggio had succeeded

Ruth, but now there was no great young power hitter coming up and the Yankee management, almost desperate, had talked Mantle out of retirement; and on September 18, 1965, they gave him a "day" in New York during which he received several thousand dollars' worth of gifts—an automobile, two quarter horses, free vacation trips to Rome, Nassau, Puerto Rico—and DiMaggio had flown to New York to make the introduction before 50,000: it had been a dramatic day, an almost holy day for the believers who had jammed the grandstands early to witness the canonization of a new stadium saint. Cardinal Spellman was on the committee, President Johnson sent a telegram, the day was officially proclaimed by the Mayor of New York, an orchestra assembled in center field in front of the trinity of monuments to Ruth, Gehrig, Huggins; and high in the grandstands, billowing in the breeze of early autumn, were white banners that read: "Don't Quit Mick," "We Love the Mick."

The banners had been held by hundreds of young boys whose dreams had been fulfilled so often by Mantle, but also seated in the grandstands were older men, paunchy and balding, in whose middle-aged minds DiMaggio was still vivid and invincible, and some of them remembered how one month before, during a pregame exhibition at Old-timers' Day in Yankee Stadium, DiMaggio had hit a pitch into the left-field seats, and suddenly thousands of people had jumped wildly to their feet, joyously screaming—the great DiMaggio had returned, they were young again, it was yesterday.

But on this sunny September day at the Stadium, the feast day of Mickey Mantle, DiMaggio was not wearing No. 5 on his back nor a black cap to cover his greying hair; he was wearing a black suit and white shirt and blue tie, and he stood in one corner of the Yankees' dugout waiting to be introduced by Red Barber, who was standing near home plate behind a silver microphone. In the outfield Guy Lombardo's Royal Canadians were playing soothing soft music; and moving slowly back and forth over the sprawling green grass between the left-field bull-pen and the infield were two carts driven by groundskeepers and containing dozens and dozens of large gifts for Mantle—a six-foot, one-hundred-pound Hebrew National salami, a Winchester rifle, a mink coat for Mrs. Mantle, a set of Wilson golf clubs, a Mercury 95-horse-power outboard motor, a Necchi portable, a year's supply of Chunky Candy. DiMaggio smoked a cigarette, but cupped it in his hands as if not wanting to be caught in the act by teen-aged boys near enough to peek down into the dugout. Then, edging forward a step, DiMaggio poked his head out and looked up. He could see nothing above except the packed towering green grandstands that seemed a mile high and moving, and he could see no clouds or blue sky, only a sky of faces. Then the announcer called out his name—*"Joe DiMaggio!"*—and suddenly there was a blast of cheering that grew louder and louder, echoing and reechoing within the big steel canyon, and DiMaggio stomped out his cigarette and climbed up the dugout steps and onto the soft green grass, the noise resounding in his ears, he could almost feel the breeze, the breath of 50,000 lungs upon him, 100,000 eyes watching his every move and for the briefest instant as he walked he closed his eyes.

Then in his path he saw Mickey Mantle's mother, a smiling elderly woman wearing an orchid, and he gently reached out for her elbow, holding it as he led her toward the microphone next to the other dignitaries lined up on the infield. Then he stood, very erect and without expression, as the cheers softened and the Stadium settled down.

Mantle was still in the dugout, in uniform, standing with one leg on the top step, and lined on both sides of him were the other Yankees who, when the ceremony was over, would play the Detroit Tigers. Then into the dugout, smiling, came Senator Robert Kennedy, accompanied by two tall curly-haired young assistants with blue eyes, Fordham freckles. Jim Farley was the first on the field to notice the Senator, and Farley muttered, loud enough for others to hear, "Who the hell invited *him?*"

Toots Shor and some of the other committeemen standing

near Farley looked into the dugout, and so did DiMaggio, his glance seeming cold, but he remaining silent. Kennedy walked up and down within the dugout shaking hands with the Yankees, but he did not walk onto the field.

"Senator," said the Yankees' manager, Johnny Keane, "why don't you sit down?" Kennedy quickly shook his head, smiled. He remained standing, and then one Yankee came over and asked about getting relatives out of Cuba, and Kennedy called over one of his aides to take down the details in a notebook.

On the infield the ceremony went on, Mantle's gifts continued to pile up—a Mobilette motor bike, a Sooner Schooner wagon barbecue, a year's supply of Chock Full O'Nuts coffee, a year's supply of Topps Chewing Gum—and the Yankee players watched, and Maris seemed glum.

"Hey, Rog," yelled a man with a tape recorder, Murray Olderman, "I want to do a thirty-second tape with you."

Maris swore angrily, shook his head.

"It'll only take a second," Olderman said.

"Why don't you ask Richardson? He's a better talker than me."

"Yes, but the fact that it comes from you. . . ."

Maris swore again. But finally he went over and said in an interview that Mantle was the finest player of his era, a great competitor, a great hitter.

Fifteen minutes later, standing behind the microphone at home plate, DiMaggio was telling the crowd, "I'm proud to introduce the man who succeeded me in center field in 1951," and from every corner of the Stadium the cheering, whistling, clapping came down. Mantle stepped forward. He stood with his wife and children, posed for the photographers kneeling in front. Then he thanked the crowd in a short speech, and, turning, shook hands with the dignitaries standing nearby. Among them now was Senator Kennedy, who had been spotted in the dugout five minutes before by Red Barber, and had been called out and introduced. Kennedy posed with Mantle for a photographer, then shook hands with the Mantle children, and with Toots Shor and James Farley and others. DiMaggio saw him coming down the line and at the last second he backed away, casually, hardly anybody noticing it, and Kennedy seemed not to notice it either, just swept past shaking more hands. . . .

FINISHING HIS TEA, putting aside the newspaper, DiMaggio went upstairs to dress, and soon he was waving good-bye to Marie and driving toward his business appointment in downtown San Francisco with his partners in the retail television business. DiMaggio, while not a millionaire, has invested wisely and has always had, since his retirement from baseball, executive positions with big companies that have paid him well. He also was among the organizers of the Fisherman's National Bank of San Francisco last year, and, though it never came about, he demonstrated an acuteness that impressed those businessmen who had thought of him only in terms of baseball. He has had offers to manage big-league baseball teams but always has rejected them, saying, "I have enough trouble taking care of my own problems without taking on the responsibilities of twenty-five ballplayers."

So his only contact with baseball these days, excluding public appearances, is his unsalaried job as a batting coach each spring in Florida with the New York Yankees, a trip he would make once again on the following Sunday, three days away, if he could accomplish what for him is always the dreaded responsibility of packing, a task made no easier by the fact that he lately has fallen into the habit of keeping his clothes in two places—some hang in his closet at home, some hang in the back room of a saloon called Reno's.

Reno's is a dimly-lit bar in the center of San Francisco. A portrait of DiMaggio swinging a bat hangs on the wall, in addition to portraits of other star athletes, and the clientele consists mainly of the sporting crowd and newspapermen, people who know DiMaggio quite well and around whom he speaks freely on a number of subjects and relaxes as he can in few other places.

The owner of the bar is Reno Barsocchini, a broadshouldered and handsome man of fifty-one with greying wavy hair who began as a fiddler in Dago Mary's tavern thirty-five years ago. He later became a bartender there and elsewhere, including Di-Maggio's Restaurant, and now he is probably DiMaggio's closest friend. He was the best man at the DiMaggio-Monroe wedding in 1954, and when they separated nine months later in Los Angeles, Reno rushed down to help DiMaggio with the packing and drive him back to San Francisco. Reno will never forget the day.

Hundreds of people were gathered around the Beverly Hills home that DiMaggio and Marilyn had rented, and photographers were perched in the trees watching the windows, and others stood on the lawn and behind the rose bushes waiting to snap pictures of anybody who walked out of the house. The newspapers that day played all the puns—"Joe Fanned on Jealousy"; "Marilyn and Joe—Out at Home"—and the Hollywood columnists, to whom DiMaggio was never an idol, never a gracious host, recounted instances of incompatibility, and Oscar Levant said it all proved that no man could be a success in two national pastimes. When Reno Barsocchini arrived he had to push his way through the mob, then bang on the door for several minutes before being admitted. Marilyn Monroe was upstairs in bed, Joe DiMaggio was downstairs with his suitcases, tense and pale, his eyes bloodshot.

Reno took the suitcases and golf clubs out to DiMaggio's car, and then DiMaggio came out of the house, the reporters moving toward him, the lights flashing.

"Where are you going?" they yelled. "I'm driving to San Francisco," he said, walking quickly.

"Is that going to be your home?"

"That *is* my home and always has been."

"Are you coming back?"

DiMaggio turned for a moment, looking up at the house.

"No," he said, "I'll never be back."

Reno Barsocchini, except for a brief falling out over something he will not discuss, has been DiMaggio's trusted companion ever since, joining him whenever he can on the golf course or on the town, otherwise waiting for him in the bar with other middle-aged men. They may wait for hours sometimes, waiting and knowing that when he arrives he may wish to be alone; but it does not seem to matter, they are endlessly awed by him, moved by the mystique, he is a kind of male Garbo. They know that he can be warm and loyal if they are sensitive to his wishes, but they must never be late for an appointment to meet him. One man, unable to find a parking place, arrived a half-hour late once and DiMaggio did not talk to him again for three months. They know, too, when dining at night with DiMaggio, that he generally prefers male companions and occasionally one or two young women, but never wives; wives gossip, wives complain, wives are trouble, and men wishing to remain close to DiMaggio must keep their wives at home.

When DiMaggio strolls into Reno's bar the men wave and call out his name, and Reno Barsocchini smiles and announces, "Here's the Clipper!," the "Yankee Clipper" being a nickname from his baseball days.

"Hey, Clipper, Clipper," Reno had said two nights before, "where you been, Clipper? . . . Clipper, how 'bout a belt?"

DiMaggio refused the offer of a drink, ordering instead a pot of tea, which he prefers to all other beverages except before a date, when he will switch to vodka.

"Hey, Joe," a sportswriter asked, a man researching a magazine piece on golf, "why is it that a golfer, when he starts getting older, loses his putting touch first? Like Snead and Hogan, they can still hit a ball well off the tee, but on the greens they lose the strokes. . . ."

"It's the pressure of age," DiMaggio said, turning around on his bar stool. "With age you get jittery. It's true of golfers, it's true of any man when he gets into his fifties. He doesn't take chances like he used to. The younger golfer, on the greens, he'll stroke his putts better. The older man, he becomes hesitant. A little uncertain. Shaky. When it comes to taking chances the younger man, even when driving a car, will take chances that the older man won't."

"Speaking of chances," another man said, one of the group that had gathered around DiMaggio, "did you see that guy on crutches in here last night?"

"Yeah, had his leg in a cast," a third said. "Skiing."

"I would never ski," DiMaggio said. "Men who ski must be doing it to impress a broad. You see these men, some of them forty, fifty, getting onto skis. And later you see them all bandaged up, broken legs. . . ."

"But skiing's a very sexy sport, Joe. All the clothes, the tight pants, the fireplace in the ski lodge, the bear rug—Christ, nobody goes to ski. They just go out there to get it cold so they can warm it up. . . ."

"Maybe you're right," DiMaggio said. "I might be persuaded."

"Want a belt, Clipper?" Reno asked.

DiMaggio thought for a second, then said, "All right—first belt tonight."

NOW IT WAS NOON, a warm sunny day. DiMaggio's business meeting with the television retailers had gone well; he had made a strong appeal to George Shahood, president of Continental Television, Inc., which has eight retail outlets in Northern California, to cut prices on color television sets and increase the sales volume, and Shahood had conceded it was worth a try. Then DiMaggio called Reno's bar to see if there were any messages, and now he was in Lefty O'Doul's car being driven along Fisherman's Wharf toward the Golden Gate Bridge en route to a golf course thirty miles upstate. Lefty O'Doul was one of the great hitters in the National League in the early Thirties, and later he managed the San Francisco Seals when DiMaggio was the shining star. Though O'Doul is now sixty-nine, eighteen years older than DiMaggio, he nevertheless possesses great energy and spirit, is a hard-drinking, boisterous man with a big belly and roving eye; and when DiMaggio, as they drove along the highway toward the golf club, noticed a lovely blonde at the wheel of a car nearby and exclaimed, "Look at *that* tomato!" O'Doul's head suddenly spun around, he took his eyes off the road, and yelled, "Where, *where?*" O'Doul's golf game is less than what it was—he used to have a two-handicap—but he still shoots in the 80's, as does DiMaggio.

DiMaggio's drives range between 250 and 280 yards when he doesn't sky them, and his putting is good, but he is distracted by a bad back that both pains him and hinders the fullness of his swing. On the first hole, waiting to tee off, DiMaggio sat back watching a foursome of college boys ahead swinging with such freedom. "Oh," he said with a sigh, "to have *their* backs."

DiMaggio and O'Doul were accompanied around the golf course by Ernie Nevers, the former football star, and two brothers who are in the hotel and movie-distribution business. They moved quickly up and down the green hills in electric golf carts, and DiMaggio's game was exceptionally good for the first nine holes. But then he seemed distracted, perhaps tired, perhaps even reacting to a conversation of a few minutes before. One of the movie men was praising the film *Boeing, Boeing,* starring Tony Curtis and Jerry Lewis, and the man asked DiMaggio if he had seen it.

"No," DiMaggio said. Then he added, swiftly, "I haven't seen a film in eight years."

DiMaggio hooked a few shots, was in the woods. He took a No. 9 iron and tried to chip out. But O'Doul interrupted DiMaggio's concentration to remind him to keep the face of the club closed. DiMaggio hit the ball. It caromed off the side of his club, went skipping like a rabbit through the high grass down toward a pond. DiMaggio rarely displays any emotion on a golf course, but now, without saying a word, he took his No. 9 iron and flung it into the air. The club landed in a tree and stayed up there.

"Well," O'Doul said, casually, "there goes *that* set of clubs."

DiMaggio walked to the tree. Fortunately the club had slipped to the lower branch and DiMaggio could stretch up on the cart and get it back.

"Every time I get advice," DiMaggio muttered to himself, shaking his head slowly and walking toward the pond, "I shank it."

Later, showered and dressed, DiMaggio and the others drove to a banquet about ten miles from the golf course. Somebody had said it was going to be an elegant dinner, but when they arrived they could see it was more like a county fair; farmers were gathered outside a big barnlike building, a candidate for sheriff was distributing leaflets at the front door, and a chorus of homely ladies were inside singing *You Are My Sunshine*.

"How did we get sucked into this?" DiMaggio asked, talking out of the side of his mouth, as they approached the building.

"O'Doul," one of the men said. "It's his fault. Damned O'Doul can't turn *anything* down."

"Go to hell," O'Doul said.

Soon DiMaggio and O'Doul and Ernie Nevers were surrounded by the crowd, and the woman who had been leading the chorus came rushing over and said, "Oh, Mr. DiMaggio, it certainly is a pleasure having you."

"It's a pleasure being here, ma'am," he said, forcing a smile.

"It's too bad you didn't arrive a moment sooner, you'd have heard our singing."

"Oh, I heard it," he said, "and I enjoyed it very much."

"Good, good," she said. "And how are your brothers Dom and Vic?"

"Fine. Dom lives near Boston. Vince is in Pittsburgh."

"Why, *hello* there, Joe," interrupted a man with wine on his breath, patting DiMaggio on the back, feeling his arm. "Who's gonna take it this year, Joe?"

"Well, I have no idea," DiMaggio said.

"What about the Giants?"

"Your guess is as good as mine."

"Well, you can't count the Dodgers out," the man said.

"You sure can't," DiMaggio said.

"Not with all that pitching."

"Pitching is certainly important," DiMaggio said.

Everywhere he goes the questions seem the same, as if he has some special vision into the future of new heroes, and everywhere he goes, too, older men grab his hand and feel his arm and predict that he could still go out there and hit one, and the smile on DiMaggio's face is genuine. He tries hard to remain as he was —he diets, he takes steam baths, he is careful; and flabby men in the locker rooms of golf clubs sometimes steal peeks at him when he steps out of the shower, observing the tight muscles across his chest, the flat stomach, the long sinewy legs. He has a young man's body, very pale and little hair; his face is dark and lined, however, parched by the sun of several seasons. Still he is always an impressive figure at banquets such as this—an *immortal,* sportswriters called him, and that is how they have written about him and others like him, rarely suggesting that such heroes might ever be prone to the ills of mortal men, carousing, drinking, scheming; to suggest this would destroy the myth, would disillusion small boys, would infuriate rich men who own ball clubs and to whom baseball is a business dedicated to profit and in pursuit of which they trade mediocre players' flesh as casually as boys trade players' pictures on bubble-gum cards. And so the baseball hero must always act the part, must preserve the myth, and none does it better than DiMaggio, none is more patient when drunken old men grab an arm and ask, "Who's gonna take it this year, Joe?"

Two hours later, dinner and the speeches over, DiMaggio is slumped in O'Doul's car headed back to San Francisco. He edged himself up, however, when O'Doul pulled into a gas station in which a pretty redhaired girl sat on a stool, legs crossed, filing her fingernails. She was about twenty-two, wore a tight black skirt and tighter white blouse.

"Look at *that,*" DiMaggio said.

"Yeah," O'Doul said.

O'Doul turned away when a young man approached, opened the gas tank, began wiping the windshield. The young man wore a greasy white uniform on the front of which was printed the name "Burt." DiMaggio kept looking at the girl, but she was not distracted from her fingernails. Then he looked at Burt, who did not recognize him. When the tank was full, O'Doul paid and drove off. Burt returned to his girl; DiMaggio slumped down in the front seat and did not open his eyes again until they'd arrived in San Francisco.

"Let's go see Reno," DiMaggio said.

"No, I gotta go see my old lady," O'Doul said. So he dropped DiMaggio off in front of the bar, and a moment later Reno's voice was announcing in the smoky room, "Hey, here's the Clipper!" The men waved and offered to buy him a drink. DiMaggio ordered a vodka and sat for an hour at the bar talking to a half dozen men around him. Then a blonde girl who had been with friends at the other end of the bar came over, and somebody introduced her to DiMaggio. He bought her a drink, offered her a cigarette. Then he struck a match and held it. His hand was unsteady.

"Is that me that's shaking?" he asked.

"It must be," said the blonde. "I'm calm."

TWO NIGHTS LATER, having collected his clothes out of Reno's back room, DiMaggio boarded a jet; he slept crossways on three seats, then came down the steps as the sun began to rise in Miami. He claimed his luggage and golf clubs, put them into the trunk of a waiting automobile, and less than an hour later he was being driven into Fort Lauderdale, past palm-lined streets, toward the Yankee Clipper Hotel.

"All my life it seems I've been on the road traveling," he said, squinting through the windshield into the sun. "I never get a sense of being in any one place."

Arriving at the Yankee Clipper Hotel, DiMaggio checked into the largest suite. People rushed through the lobby to shake hands with him, to ask for his autograph, to say, "Joe, you look great." And early the next morning, and for the next thirty mornings, DiMaggio arrived punctually at the baseball park and wore his uniform with the famous No. 5, and the tourists seated in the sunny grandstands clapped when he first appeared on the field each time, and then they watched with nostalgia as he picked up a bat and played "pepper" with the younger Yankees, some of whom were not even born when, twenty-five years ago this summer, he hit in fifty-six straight games and became the most celebrated man in America.

But the younger spectators in the Fort Lauderdale park, and the sportswriters, too, were more interested in Mantle and Maris, and nearly every day there were news dispatches reporting how Mantle and Maris felt, what they did, what they said, even though they said and did very little except walk around the field frowning when photographers asked for another picture and when sportswriters asked how they felt.

After seven days of this, the big day arrived—Mantle and Maris would swing a bat—and a dozen sportswriters were gathered around the big batting cage that was situated beyond the left-field fence; it was completely enclosed in wire, meaning that no baseball could travel more than thirty or forty feet before being trapped in rope; still Mantle and Maris would be swinging, and this, in spring, makes news.

Mantle stepped in first. He wore black gloves to help prevent blisters. He hit right-handed against the pitching of a coach named Vern Benson, and soon Mantle was swinging hard, smashing line drives against the nets, going *ahhh ahhh* as he followed through with his mouth open.

Then Mantle, not wanting to overdo it on his first day, dropped his bat in the dirt and walked out of the batting cage. Roger Maris stepped in. He picked up Mantle's bat.

"This damn thing must be thirty-eight ounces." Maris said. He threw the bat down into the dirt, left the cage and walked toward the dugout on the other side of the field to get a lighter bat.

DiMaggio stood among the sportswriters behind the cage, then turned when Vern Benson, inside the cage, yelled, "Joe, wanna hit some?"

"No chance," DiMaggio said.

"Com'on, Joe," Benson said.

The reporters waited silently. Then DiMaggio walked slowly into the cage and picked up Mantle's bat. He took his position at the plate but obviously it was not the classic DiMaggio stance; he was holding the bat about two inches from the knob, his feet were not so far apart, and, when DiMaggio took a cut at Benson's first pitch, fouling it, there was none of that ferocious follow through, the blurred bat did not come whipping all the way around, the No. 5 was not stretched full across his broad back.

DiMaggio fouled Benson's second pitch, then he connected solidly with the third, the fourth, the fifth. He was just meeting the ball easily, however, not smashing it, and Benson called out. "I didn't know you were a choke hitter, Joe."

"I am now," DiMaggio said, getting ready for another pitch.

He hit three more squarely enough, and then he swung again and there was a hollow sound.

"Ohhh," DiMaggio yelled, dropping his bat, his fingers stung, "I was waiting for that one." He left the batting cage rubbing his hands together. The reporters watched him. Nobody said anything. Then DiMaggio said to one of them, not in anger nor in sadness, but merely as a simply stated fact, "There was a time when you couldn't get me out of there."

I generally suggest nonfiction of that character and quality as a model for the fiction writer chiefly because I think it makes an important point dramatically: *You cannot write well without data* (I have an additional and specific reason for using Talese's work, which I will get to later on). Nobody else can, either, regardless of whether his or her purpose is nonfiction or fiction.

That is why so many of the most interesting fiction writers prove on scrutiny to be reporters who have gone straight. While I do not think it is mandatory that a prospective fiction writer submit to a period of indentured servitude as a reporter, I do think that kind of background is a substantial advantage. The best writing school in the world, in my estimation, is the one that has branches in every major city on the globe; it is called the Associated Press. The A.P. does not allow its reporters and rewritemen to make up the stories, and fires the ones it catches in the act of doing that, but it does teach its scribblers to get it fast, get it right, write it down, and send it out. Nobody at A.P. suffers from writer's block, not for long, anyway; stubborn cases decline quickly into seizures of terminal unemployment. Nobody at A.P. has more than an occasional mild case of logorrhea, or is perpetually overdrawn at the adjectival and adverbial bank. The lines of transmission are crowded; there is no room on them for a lot of fancy showing off. The deadline is every minute, because somewhere in the world one of A.P.'s members is going to press, or on the air; most of them subscribe to other, even more expensive news services as well, and can be depended upon to bitch loudly if A.P. seems to force the extravagance by trailing the opposition. If you want to learn how to keep your short fiction to three thousand words and how to write books in obedience to the bank robber's rule—Get In. Get the Money. Get Out.—and your ego and your bankroll seem up to enduring the pressure, wheedle yourself into a job as a reporter for the Associated Press.

Failing that, read nonfiction carefully. Solid reportage is interesting precisely because the reporter has gone to the trouble of acquiring information about his or her subject, and then has carefully organized it, so that the reader completing the text knows something that he or she did not know before. James Reston, reflecting on his long and distinguished career as a reporter and commentator on national politics for *The*

New York Times, concluded that any respect he deserved was probably attributable to his early experience as a sportswriter. To cover sports, he said, the reporter soon learns that he must pay attention at all times, because no one ever becomes sufficiently expert to predict unerringly the outcome of every contest. The rookie who begins by covering politics and government does not invariably receive that salutary instruction, and therefore becomes easy prey to the delusion that he or she is an expert who need not watch and listen carefully to acquire the story. People who read the sports pages are usually more demanding than the people who read political pundits; they have something specific in mind when they open the paper to read about the ball game. They already know it was played. They may know how it came out, but the reporter can't assume that. Neither can the reporter rest content with a mere statement of that outcome; the fans expect an account of how it came about, and some explanation, too. Most of them have a fair amount of background information about the sport itself and the people who play it. Many of them have a great deal of information, and are only too triumphantly pleased to volunteer corrections when the reporter gets it wrong. When the reporter is promoted to writing a column about sports, it is usually with the understanding that mere opinions on the topic of the day will not suffice; those opinions will be taken seriously only if they are manifestly grounded in fact. It is fairly easy for a political commentator to get away with a little coasting, and write a bellyscratcher now and then, when he is off his feed and indolence seems more appealing than honest industry. Political columnists are understood to be soothsayers, and not held to a standard of reliability even as modest as that which Clocker Dan's tip-sheet customers expect him to meet touting racetrack winners each day. Sports columnists do not enjoy such latitude. When they get it wrong, there is all hell to pay.

Talese, when he began writing the *Esquire* pieces, paid the same respect to the readers of his magazine work that he accorded to those who read him in the *Times*. He continued that practice when he wrote a book about the *Times*, *The Kingdom and the Power*, published in 1968, to the reported consternation of some of his former employers (its success was his publisher's motive for collecting the *Esquire* pieces); when he wrote *Honor Thy Father*, his 1971 study of the Bonanno branch of the Mafia, which failed to elate many hoods; and when he wrote *Thy Neighbor's Wife*, the 1980 report on the pre-AIDS-and-herpes status of the sexual revolution, which he researched with truly remarkable diligence, reportedly to the discomfort of his wife.

The fiction writer owes that same debt of respect to the reader. Talese is a particularly worthy exemplar for the fiction writer because, as he said in his Author's Note to the collection, his *Esquire* work showed "early signs of my interest in using the techniques of fiction, an aspiration on my part to somehow bring to reportage the tone that Irwin Shaw and John O'Hara had brought to the short story." If you read Talese's nonfiction carefully, you can learn a lot about writing fiction (you may even suffer the temptation to write nonfiction instead of making up your stories, and you should succumb at once if you do: nonfiction generally pays a lot better).

There are numerous other nonfiction books that I recommend strongly to prospective writers of fiction (and I'm glad there are a lot of them, because the fiction writers that I know practice the same sort of creative celibacy I observe when engaged in writing fiction: I don't read anybody else's, for fear of unintentional imitation, but I really do need something to read). Truman Capote's *In Cold Blood*, Norman Mailer's *The Executioner's Song*, Tom Wolfe's *The Right Stuff*, David Eisenhower's *Eisenhower*, Roger Angell's collections of his baseball pieces for *The New Yorker*, David McCullough's *Mornings on Horseback*, Ronald Steel's *Walter Lippmann and the American Century,* A. M. Sperber's *Murrow,* John Keegan's *The Mask of Command,* Garrett Mattingly's *The Armada,* Lord David Cecil's *Melbourne;* those are books chosen at random from a catalogue of history and biography that has nurtured me through years of virtuous fiction writing.

Among my special favorites are the works of William Manchester. His biography of H. L. Mencken, *Disturber of the Peace* (first published in 1951, with a second edition twenty-five years later) introduced me to his work, and I followed it faithfully thereafter. I missed *A Rockefeller Family Portrait,* but like most of the rest of America's readers, I devoured *American Caesar, The Death of a President, The Arms of Krupp,* and *The Glory and the Dream.*

Lassitude and the apprehension of seeming presumptuous prevented me until 1980 from writing to this stranger to thank him for the extraordinary pleasure his hard work had given to me. But that year *Goodbye, Darkness: A Memoir of the Pacific War* was published, and my admiration overcame my reticence. It is just what he calls it: not a history and not a novel, either, but a recollection of how it *felt* to be a marine in World War II. It is also a striking example of the way that observation germinates in the memory until it produces a vision so clear and so symmetrical that it has to be written down. Since that is how fiction comes about, I think a person wishing to write it for money ought to read *Goodbye, Darkness* and watch it happening. This is the preamble.

Our Boeing 747 has been fleeing westward from darkened California, racing across the Pacific toward the sun, the incandescent eye of God, but slowly, three hours later than West Coast time, twilight gathers outside, veil upon lilac veil. This is what the French call *l'heure bleue.* Aquamarine becomes turquoise; turquoise, lavendar; lavendar, violet; violet, magenta; magenta, mulberry. Seen through my cocktail glass, the light fades as it deepens; it becomes opalescent, crepuscular. In the last waning moments of the day I can still feel the failing sunlight on my cheek, taste it in my martini. The plane rises before a spindrift; the darkening sky, broken by clouds like combers, boils and foams overhead. Then the whole weight of evening falls upon me. Old memories, phantoms repressed for more than a third of a century, begin to stir. I can almost hear the rhythm of surf on distant snow-white beaches. I have another drink, and then I learn, for the hundredth time, that you can't drown your troubles, not the real ones, because if they are real they can swim. One of my worst recollections, one I had buried in my deepest memory bank long ago, comes back with a clarity so blinding that I surge forward against the seat belt, appalled by it, filled with remorse and shame.

I am remembering the first man I slew.

THERE WAS this little hut on Motobu, perched atop a low rise overlooking the East China Sea. It was a fisherman's shack, so ordinary that scarcely anyone had noticed it. I did. I noticed it because I happened to glance in that direction at a crucial moment. The hut lay between us and B Company of the First Battalion. Word had been passed that that company had been taking sniper losses. They thought the sharpshooters were in spider holes, Jap foxholes, but as I was looking that way, I saw two B Company guys drop, and from the angle of their fall I knew the firing had to come from a window on the other side of that hut. At the same time, I saw that the shack had windows on *our* side, which meant that once the rifleman had B Company pinned down, he could turn toward us. I was dug in with Barney Cobb. We had excellent defilade ahead and the Twenty-second Marines on our right flank, but we had no protection from the hut, and our hole wasn't deep enough to let us sweat it out. Every time I glanced at that shack I was looking into the empty eye socket of death.

The situation was as clear as the deduction from a euclidean theorem, but my psychological state was extremely complicated. S. L. A. Marshall once observed that the typical fighting man is often at a disadvantage because he "comes from a civilization in which aggression, connected with the taking of life, is prohibited and unacceptable." This was especially true of me, whose horror of violence had been so deep-seated that I had been unable to trade punches with other boys. But since then life had become cheaper to me. "Two thousand pounds of education drops to a ten rupee," wrote Kipling of the fighting on India's North-West Frontier. My plight was not unlike that described by the famous sign in the Paris zoo: "Warning: this animal is vicious; when attacked, it defends itself." I was responding to a basic biological principle first set down by the German zoologist Heini Hediger in his *Skizzen zu einer Tierpsychologie um und im Zirkus.* Hediger noted that beyond a certain distance, which varies from one species to another, an animal will retreat, while within it, it will attack. He called these "flight distance" and "critical distance." Obviously I was within critical distance of the hut. It was time to bar the bridge, stick a finger in the dike— to do *something.* I could be quick or I could be dead.

My choices were limited. Moving inland was inconvenient; the enemy was there, too. I was on the extreme left of our perimeter, and somehow I couldn't quite see myself turning my back on the shack and fleeing through the rest of the battalion screaming, like Chicken Little, "A Jap's after me! A Jap's after me!" Of course, I could order one of my people to take out the sniper; but I played the role of the NCO in Kipling's poem who always looks after the black sheep, and if I ducked this one, they would never let me forget it. Also, I couldn't be certain that the order would be obeyed. I was a gangling, long-boned youth, wholly lacking in what the Marine Corps called "command presence"—charisma—and I led nineteen highly insubordinate men. I couldn't even be sure that Barney would budge. It is war, not politics, that makes strange bedfellows. The fact that I outranked Barney was in itself odd. He was a great blond buffalo of a youth, with stubby hair, a scraggly mustache, and a powerful build. Before the war he had swum breaststroke for Brown, and had left me far behind in two intercollegiate meets. I valued his respect for me, which cowardice would have wiped out. So I asked him if he had any grenades. He didn't; nobody in the section did. The grenade shortage was chronic. That sterile exchange bought a little time, but every moment lengthened my odds against the Nip sharpshooter. Finally, sweating with the greatest fear I had known till then, I took a deep breath, told Barney, "Cover me," and took off for the hut at Mach 2 speed in little bounds, zigzagging and dropping every dozen steps, remembering to roll as I dropped. I was nearly there, arrowing in, when I realized that I wasn't wearing my steel helmet. The only cover on my head was my cloth Raider cap. That was a violation of orders. I was out of uniform. I remember hoping, idiotically, that nobody would report me.

Utterly terrified, I jolted to a stop on the threshold of the shack. I could feel a twitching in my jaw, coming and going like a winky light signaling some disorder. Various valves were opening and closing in my stomach. My mouth was dry, my legs quaking, and my eyes out of focus. Then my vision cleared. I unlocked the safety of my Colt, kicked the door with my right foot, and leapt inside. My horror returned. I was in an empty room. There was another door opposite the one I had unhinged, which meant another room, which meant the sniper was in there— and had been warned by the crash of the outer door. But I had committed myself. Flight was impossible now. So I smashed into the other room and saw him as a blur to my right. I wheeled that way, crouched, gripped the pistol butt in both hands, and fired.

Not only was he the first Japanese soldier I had ever shot at; he was the only one I had seen at close quarters. He was a robin-fat, moon-faced, roly-poly little man with his thick, stubby, trunklike legs sheathed in faded khaki puttees and the rest of him squeezed into a uniform that was much too tight. Unlike me, he was wearing a tin hat, dressed to kill. But I was quite safe from him. His Arisaka rifle was strapped on in a sniper's harness, and though he had heard me, and was trying to turn toward me, the harness sling had him trapped. He couldn't disentangle himself from it. His eyes were rolling in panic. Realizing that he couldn't extricate his arms and defend himself, he was backing toward a corner with a curious, crablike motion.

My first shot had missed him, embedding itself in the straw wall, but the second caught him dead-on in the femoral artery. His left thigh blossomed, swiftly turning to mush. A wave of blood gushed from the wound; then another boiled out, sheeting across his legs, pooling on the earthen floor. Mutely he looked down at it. He dipped a hand in it and listlessly smeared his cheek red. His shoulders gave a little spasmodic jerk, as though someone had whacked him on the back; then he emitted a tremendous, raspy fart, slumped down, and died. I kept firing, wasting government property.

Already I thought I detected the dark brown effluvium of the freshly slain, a sour, pervasive emanation which is different from anything else you have known. Yet seeing death at that range, like smelling it, requires no previous experience. You instantly recognize the spastic convulsion and the rattle, which in his case was not loud, but deprecating and conciliatory, like the manners of civilian Japanese. He continued to sink until he reached the earthen floor. His eyes glazed over. Almost immediately a fly landed on his left eyeball. It was joined by another. I don't know how long I stood there staring. I knew from previous combat what lay ahead for the corpse. It would swell, then bloat, bursting out of the uniform. Then the face would turn from yellow to red, to purple, to green, to black. My father's account of the Argonne had omitted certain vital facts. A feeling of disgust and self-hatred clotted darkly in my throat, gagging me.

Jerking my head to shake off the stupor, I slipped a new, fully loaded magazine into the butt of my .45. Then I began to tremble, and next to shake, all over. I sobbed, in a voice still grainy with fear: "I'm sorry." Then I threw up all over myself. I recognized the half-digested C-ration beans dribbling down my front, smelled the vomit above the cordite. At the same time I noticed another odor; I had urinated in my skivvies. I pondered fleetingly why our excretions become so loathsome the instant they leave the body. Then Barney burst in on me, his carbine at the ready, his face gray, as though he, not I, had just become a partner in the firm of death. He ran over to the Nip's body, grabbed its stacking swivel—its neck—and let go, satisfied that it was a cadaver. I marveled at his courage; I couldn't have taken a step toward that corner. He approached me and then backed away, in revulsion, from my foul stench. He said: "Slim, you stink." I said nothing. I knew I had become a thing of tears and twitchings and dirtied pants. I remember wondering dumbly: *Is this what they mean by "conspicuous gallantry"?*

None of what I have offered so far is intended to suggest that the person who proposes to write good fiction for money should intrude upon Joe DiMaggio, or enlist to fight in the next available war. The purpose is instead to propose the possibility that the prospective professional writer's data are right before his eyes, and need only shaping to acquire story status.

It seems to me that Talese's stated intention—to adapt the methods of such fictional story masters as John O'Hara and Irwin Shaw to the necessities of nonfiction—and Manchester's accomplishment in transforming the empirical, but recollected, experience of combat into an account truer than the facts could be, together provide a legitimate transition to the achievement of the synthesis of reality and imagination that makes a story.

I think it was significant that Talese mentioned only O'Hara and Shaw as his sources of technique. There are many writers still around who rival them in the expert transformation of experience into story—my friend Ward Just is only one; if you would like to read a wonderful story, search out "The Congressman Who Loved Flaubert"—and they excel in utilizing the quotidian event as the linchpin of the tale (O'Hara, the master, gets his full innings later on). Shaw is just a little bit easier to track, making an incident into a round story, and therefore a better choice to demonstrate the conversion of an ordinary incident in an ordinary life into a story that once made simply stands there and exists. I had the devil's own time selecting one of Shaw's—I don't feel bad about that; his introduction to *Short Stories: Five Decades* contains this rueful admission: "Originally this book was intended to contain all of my stories, but when the count was made the total came to eighty-four, and to include them all would have meant a formidably bulky and outrageous book. Since my publishers and I agreed that we did not wish to produce a book that the reader could neither carry nor afford, we fixed on sixty-three as a reasonable number and began the sad process of winnowing out the ones we would leave behind." The culling left 756 pages of extraordinary work.

Nobody ever had better titles than Irwin Shaw did. "God Was Here but He Left Early." "Sailor off the Bremen." "Night in Algiers." "A Year to Learn the Language." "Tip on a Dead Jockey." And that justifiable favorite of anthology editors: "The Eighty-Yard Run." I caved in to my own preference and chose "The Girls in Their Summer Dresses." Read this aloud and think about how many pedestrian, awkward days and nights you have spent with someone that you really cared about, and hurt without meaning to, and how many stories you already know, but haven't yet written down.

Fifth Avenue was shining in the sun when they left the Brevoort and started walking toward Washington Square. The sun was warm, even though it was November and everything looked like

Sunday morning—the buses, and the well-dressed people walking slowly in couples and the quiet buildings with the windows closed.

Michael held Frances' arm tightly as they walked downtown in the sunlight. They walked lightly, almost smiling, because they had slept late and had a good breakfast and it was Sunday. Michael unbuttoned his coat and let it flap around him in the mild wind. They walked, without saying anything, among the young and pleasant-looking people who somehow seem to make up most of the population of that section of New York City.

"Look out," Frances said, as they crossed Eighth Street. "You'll break your neck."

Michael laughed and Frances laughed with him.

"She's not so pretty, anyway," Frances said. "Anyway, not pretty enough to take a chance breaking your neck looking at her."

Michael laughed again. He laughed louder this time, but not as solidly. "She wasn't a bad-looking girl. She had a nice complexion. Country-girl complexion. How did you know I was looking at her?"

Frances cocked her head to one side and smiled at her husband under the tip-tilted brim of her hat. "Mike, darling . . ." she said.

Michael laughed, just a little laugh this time. "O.K.," he said. "The evidence is in. Excuse me. It was the complexion. It's not the sort of complexion you see much in New York. Excuse me."

Frances patted his arm lightly and pulled him along a little faster toward Washington Square.

"This is a nice morning," she said. "This is a wonderful morning. When I have breakfast with you it makes me feel good all day."

"Tonic," Michael said. "Morning pick-up. Rolls and coffee with Mike and you're on the alkali side, guaranteed."

"That's the story. Also, I slept all night, wound around you like a rope."

"Saturday night," he said. "I permit such liberties only when the week's work is done."

"You're getting fat," she said.

"Isn't it the truth? The lean man from Ohio."

"I love it," she said, "an extra five pounds of husband."

"I love it, too," Michael said gravely.

"I have an idea," Frances said.

"My wife has an idea. That pretty girl."

"Let's not see anybody all day," Frances said. "Let's just hang around with each other. You and me. We're always up to our neck in people, drinking their Scotch, or drinking our Scotch, we only see each other in bed . . ."

"The Great Meeting Place," Michael said. "Stay in bed long enough and everybody you ever knew will show up there."

"Wise guy," Frances said. "I'm talking serious."

"O.K., I'm listening serious."

"I want to go out with my husband all day long. I want him to talk only to me and listen only to me."

"What's to stop us?" Michael asked. "What party intends to prevent me from seeing my wife alone on Sunday? What party?"

"The Stevensons. They want us to drop by around one o'clock and they'll drive us into the country."

"The lousy Stevensons," Mike said. "Transparent. They can whistle. They can go driving in the country by themselves. My wife and I have to stay in New York and bore each other tête-à-tête."

"Is it a date?"

"It's a date."

Frances leaned over and kissed him on the tip of the ear.

"Darling," Michael said. "This is Fifth Avenue."

"Let me arrange a program," Frances said. "A planned Sunday in New York for a young couple with money to throw away."

"Go easy."

"First let's go see a football game. A professional football game," Frances said, because she knew Michael loved to watch them. "The Giants are playing. And it'll be nice to be outside all day today and get hungry and later we'll go down to Cavanagh's and get a steak as big as a blacksmith's apron, with a bottle of wine, and after that, there's a new French picture at the Filmarte that everybody says . . . Say, are you listening to me?"

"Sure," he said. He took his eyes off the hatless girl with the dark hair, cut dancer-style, like a helmet, who was walking past him with the self-conscious strength and grace dancers have. She was walking without a coat and she looked very solid and strong and her belly was flat, like a boy's, under her skirt, and her hips swung boldly because she was a dancer and also because she knew Michael was looking at her. She smiled a little to herself as she went past and Michael noticed all these things before he looked back at his wife. "Sure," he said, "we're going to watch the Giants and we're going to eat steak and we're going to see a French picture. How do you like that?"

"That's it," Frances said flatly. "That's the program for the day. Or maybe you'd just rather walk up and down Fifth Avenue."

"No," Michael said carefully. "Not at all."

"You always look at other women," Frances said. "At every damn woman in the City of New York."

"Oh, come now," Michael said, pretending to joke. "Only pretty ones. And, after all, how many pretty women *are* there in New York? Seventeen?"

"More. At least you seem to think so. Wherever you go."

"Not the truth. Occasionally, maybe, I look at a woman as she passes. In the street. I admit, perhaps in the street I look at a woman once in a while . . ."

"Everywhere," Frances said. "Every damned place we go. Restaurants, subways, theaters, lectures, concerts."

"Now, darling," Michael said, "I look at everything. God gave me eyes and I look at women and men and subway excavations and moving pictures and the little flowers of the field. I casually inspect the universe."

"You ought to see the look in your eye," Frances said, "as you casually inspect the universe on Fifth Avenue."

"I'm a happily married man." Michael pressed her elbow tenderly, knowing what he was doing. "Example for the whole twentieth century, Mr. and Mrs. Mike Loomis."

"You mean it?"

"Frances, baby . . ."

"Are you *really* happily married?"

"Sure," Michael said, feeling the whole Sunday morning sinking like lead inside him. "Now what the hell is the sense in talking like that?"

"I would like to know." Frances walked faster now, looking straight ahead, her face showing nothing, which was the way she always managed it when she was arguing or feeling bad.

"I'm wonderfully happily married," Michael said patiently. "I am the envy of all men between the ages of fifteen and sixty in the State of New York."

"Stop kidding," Frances said.

"I have a fine home," Michael said. "I got nice books and a phonograph and nice friends. I live in a town I like the way I like and I do the work I like and I live with the woman I like. Whenever something good happens, don't I run to you? When something bad happens, don't I cry on your shoulder?"

"Yes," Frances said. "You look at every woman that passes."

"That's an exaggeration."

"Every woman." Frances took her hand off Michael's arm. "If she's not pretty you turn away fairly quickly. If she's halfway pretty you watch her for about seven steps . . ."

"My lord, Frances!"

"If she's pretty you practically break your neck . . ."

"Hey, let's have a drink," Michael said, stopping.

"We just had breakfast."

"Now, listen, darling," Mike said, choosing his words with care, "it's a nice day and we both feel good and there's no reason why we have to break it up. Let's have a nice Sunday."

"I could have a fine Sunday if you didn't look as though you were dying to run after every skirt on Fifth Avenue."

"Let's have a drink," Michael said.

"I don't want a drink."

"What do you want, a fight?"

"No," Frances said so unhappily that Michael felt terribly sorry for her. "I don't want a fight. I don't know why I started this. All right, let's drop it. Let's have a good time."

They joined hands consciously and walked without talking among the baby carriages and the old Italian men in their Sunday clothes and the young women with Scotties in Washington Square Park.

"I hope it's a good game today," Frances said after a while, her tone a good imitation of the tone she had used at breakfast and at the beginning of their walk. "I like professional football games. They hit each other as though they're made out of concrete. When they tackle each other," she said, trying to make Michael laugh, "they make divots. It's very exciting."

"I want to tell you something," Michael said very seriously. "I have not touched another woman. Not once. In all the five years."

"All right," Frances said.

"You believe that, don't you?"

"All right."

They walked between the crowded benches, under the scrubby city park trees.

"I try not to notice it," Frances said, as though she were talking to herself. "I try to make believe it doesn't mean anything. Some men're like that, I tell myself, they have to see what they're missing."

"Some women're like that, too," Michael said. "In my time I've seen a couple of ladies."

"I haven't even looked at another man," Frances said, walking straight ahead, "since the second time I went out with you."

"There's no law," Michael said.

"I feel rotten inside, in my stomach, when we pass a woman and you look at her and I see that look in your eye and that's the way you looked at me the first time, in Alice Maxwell's house. Standing there in the living room, next to the radio, with a green hat on and all those people."

"I remember the hat," Michael said.

"The same look," Frances said. "And it makes me feel bad. It makes me feel terrible."

"Sssh, please, darling, sssh . . ."

"I think I would like a drink now," Frances said.

They walked over to a bar on Eighth Street, not saying anything, Michael automatically helping her over curbstones, and guiding her past automobiles. He walked, buttoning his coat, looking thoughtfully at his neatly shined heavy brown shoes as they made the steps toward the bar. They sat near a window in the bar and the sun streamed in, and there was a small cheerful fire in the fireplace. A little Japanese waiter came over and put down some pretzels and smiled happily at them.

"What do you order after breakfast?" Michael asked.

"Brandy, I suppose," Frances said.

"Courvoisier," Michael told the waiter. "Two Courvoisier."

The waiter came with the glasses and they sat drinking the brandy, in the sunlight. Michael finished half his and drank a little water.

"I look at women," he said. "Correct. I don't say it's wrong or right, I look at them. If I pass them on the street and I don't look at them, I'm fooling you, I'm fooling myself."

"You look at them as though you want them," Frances said, playing with her brandy glass. "Every one of them."

"In a way," Michael said, speaking softly and not to his wife, "in a way that's true. I don't do anything about it, but it's true."

"I know it. That's why I feel bad."

"Another brandy," Michael called. "Waiter, two more brandies."

"Why do you hurt me?" Frances asked. "What're you doing?"

Michael sighed and closed his eyes and rubbed them gently with his fingertips. "I love the way women look. One of the things I like best about New York is the battalions of women. When I first came to New York from Ohio that was the first thing I noticed, the million wonderful women, all over the city. I walked around with my heart in my throat."

"A kid," Frances said. "That's a kid's feeling."

"Guess again," Michael said. "Guess again. I'm older now, I'm a man getting near middle age, putting on a little fat and I still love to walk along Fifth Avenue at three o'clock on the east side of the street between Fiftieth and Fifty-seventh Streets, they're all out then, making believe they're shopping, in their furs and their crazy hats, everything all concentrated from all over the world into eight blocks, the best furs, the best clothes, the handsomest women, out to spend money and feeling good about it, looking coldly at you, making believe they're not looking at you as you go past."

The Japanese waiter put the two drinks down, smiling with great happiness.

"Everything is all right?" he asked.

"Everything is wonderful," Michael said.

"If it's just a couple of fur coats," Frances said, "and forty-five-dollar hats . . ."

"It's not the fur coats. Or the hats. That's just the scenery for that particular kind of woman. Understand," he said, "you don't have to listen to this."

"I want to listen."

"I like the girls in the offices. Neat, with their eyeglasses, smart, chipper, knowing what everything is about, taking care of themselves all the time." He kept his eye on the people going slowly past outside the window. "I like the girls on Forty-fourth Street at lunch time, the actresses, all dressed up on nothing a week, talking to the good-looking boys, wearing themselves out being young and vivacious outside Sardi's, waiting for producers to look at them. I like the salesgirls in Macy's, paying attention to you first because you're a man, leaving lady customers waiting, flirting with you over socks and books and phonograph needles. I got all this stuff accumulated in me because I've been thinking about it for ten years and now you've asked for it and here it is."

"Go ahead," Frances said.

"When I think of New York City, I think of all the girls, the Jewish girls, the Italian girls, the Irish, Polack, Chinese, German, Negro, Spanish, Russian girls, all on parade in the city. I don't know whether it's something special with me or whether every man in the city walks around with the same feeling inside him, but I feel as though I'm at a picnic in this city. I like to sit near the women in the theaters, the famous beauties who've taken six hours to get ready and look it. And the young girls at the football games, with the red cheeks, and when the warm weather comes, the girls in their summer dresses . . ." He finished his drink. "That's the story. You asked for it, remember. I can't help but look at them. I can't help but want them."

"You want them," Frances repeated without expression. "You said that."

"Right," Michael said, being cruel now and not caring, because she had made him expose himself. "You brought this subject up for discussion, we will discuss it fully."

Frances finished her drink and swallowed two or three times extra. "You say you love me?"

"I love you, but I also want them. O.K."

"I'm pretty, too," Frances said. "As pretty as any of them."

"You're beautiful," Michael said, meaning it.

"I'm good for you," Frances said, pleading. "I've made a good wife, a good housekeeper, a good friend. I'd do any damn thing for you."

"I know," Michael said. He put his hand out and grasped hers.

"You'd like to be free to . . ." Frances said.

"Sssh."

"Tell the truth." She took her hand away from under his.

Michael flicked the edge of his glass with his finger. "O.K.," he said gently. "Sometimes I feel I would like to be free."

"Well," Frances said defiantly, drumming on the table, "anytime you say . . ."

"Don't be foolish." Michael swung his chair around to her side of the table and patted her thigh.

She began to cry, silently, into her handkerchief, bent over just enough so that nobody else in the bar would notice. "Some day," she said, crying, "you're going to make a move . . ."

Michael didn't say anything. He sat watching the bartender slowly peel a lemon.

"Aren't you?" Frances asked harshly. "Come on, tell me. Talk. Aren't you?"

"Maybe," Michael said. He moved his chair back again. "How the hell do I know?"

"You know," Frances persisted. "Don't you know?"

"Yes," Michael said after a while, "I know."

Frances stopped crying then. Two or three snuffles into the handkerchief and she put it away and her face didn't tell anything to anybody. "At least do me one favor," she said.

"Sure."

"Stop talking about how pretty this woman is, or that one. Nice eyes, nice breasts, a pretty figure, good voice," she mimicked his voice. "Keep it to yourself. I'm not interested."

"Excuse me." Michael waved to the waiter. "I'll keep it to myself."

Frances flicked the corner of her eyes. "Another brandy," she told the waiter.

"Two," Michael said.

"Yes, ma'am, yes, sir," said the waiter, backing away.

Frances regarded him coolly across the table. "Do you want me to call the Stevensons?" she asked. "It'll be nice in the country."

"Sure," Michael said. "Call them up."

She got up from the table and walked across the room toward

the telephone. Michael watched her walk, thinking, what a pretty girl, what nice legs.

The similarities among the three pieces you have just read —the first a stellar piece of reportage; the second a day in combat recollected in tranquillity; the third in its terse way what seems at least to me to be the regretful reflection of a man who sorrowed before the fact, and continued afterward to do so, in his willful destruction of a working marriage to a good woman—do more than illustrate the mysterious process of converting what has been seen and heard into lasting fiction. That, from the writer's point of view, would be entirely sufficient, but there is more to be garnered than that.

Each of the pieces begins in virtually the same way: "It was not quite spring," Talese tells us, "the silent season before the search for salmon, and the old fishermen of San Francisco were either painting their boats or repairing their nets along the pier or sitting in the sun talking quietly among themselves, watching the tourists come and go, and smiling, now, as a pretty girl paused to take their picture." That is a long sentence, as long as a train that seems to take forever to pass between the black-and-white-striped wooden gates barring the railroad tracks that cross a country road, but it needs to be because it too carries a lot of freight. It sets the elegiac tone for what is to be a reflection on a theme that Talese craftily never makes explicit: the transience of what appears to be, at the time of its occurrence, permanent fame. The young girl with the camera does not understand the most-likely-lascivious comments made by the old fishermen, because she does not speak Sicilian. And she does not notice the man with the gray hair gazing at her from the window because she knows no reason why she should; perhaps unjustly Talese has made it clear he thinks the girl is egotistically accustomed to having older men stare at her hungrily, and has learned to pay no heed unless she has her own reason for doing so.

Manchester puts you right on the plane with him. This is prose that hits with the force of a blackjack, the cadence of the sentences mimicking the pitch and yaw of an aircraft in flight that keep the inner ears on sentinel alert, and the muscles tensing and relaxing to compensate for shifts of angle, the tumbling and disoriented images falling away into the second paragraph, one sentence that explains that more is going on here than the customary effort of a reluctant traveler to endure with equanimity a flight he did not wish to take. He is thinking about the *first* man that he killed. So we are to understand that he killed others after that, who were trying to kill him, and that since we are not told at once what strong emotions followed those events, their deaths came easier to him.

Shaw's Michael Loomis, so far as we will ever know, has never experienced a night in bed with Marilyn Monroe, thinking it would last forever, or killed a man who was equally determined to kill him. But on Fifth Avenue in New York on a November Sunday, at the prodding of his wife, he arrives at what is probably an understanding of himself that he has suppressed for a long time. It is not good news, and he wishes already that he were not doomed to do what he now knows he will do, but that is no help now; he knows it, and he will do it, and he will wish he hadn't.

The commonality of these pieces of writing is the oblique approach they take to a subject that none of them ever states directly. In each instance, the writer takes good care to situate his reader in the context of his protagonist, and allows— indeed, requires—the reader to deduce from the data provided what has happened to his hero that merits narration of his story. You know at once where you are, and who is your companion, and why you should be interested in what happens to him. That is entirely good enough, and quite obediently you proceed from the actual man who played center field for the Yankees to the aging man who killed as a raw youth in the Pacific to the man of early middle age who discovers in New York on an autumn Sunday that sooner or later he is certain to betray his wife's trust, and knows it just as surely as she does, utterly unconcerned by such ancillary issues as whether what you read is fact or fiction.

That is the first and minor secret of getting your story or book published: Never tell your reader what your story is about. Reading is a participatory sport. People do it because they are intelligent and enjoy figuring things out for themselves. If you are smart enough to perceive a story lurking in Joe DiMaggio's contemplation of a pretty girl through a restaurant window, and you are cocksure enough to think that small epiphany contains a legend that a stranger would enjoy knowing, then you replicate it for him, in prose, and allow him to see it for himself.

The second, major secret is that there is no secret. First you have to learn to write. Then you have to acquire the story; the data are the raw material. Then you have to write the story, and produce a clean manuscript of it. Then you send it out, with packaging and postage for what will most likely prove to be its inevitable reappearance. That usually occurs at the end of a day that has already been entirely bad enough to suit anyone this side of a prisoner on Death Row whose appeal for commutation of sentence has been denied. It is no good feeling sorry for yourself. That, as John O'Hara would say, is a mug's game. We all know it's hard work. Nobody asked any one of us to become a writer. No one will care if you don't become one.

No one but you, that is.

4

Fiction is not a competitive sport.
–John Cheever

The problem that bedevils students in writing classes is that it is so hard to write fiction to order. And the problem, equally frustrating, that baffles people who are trying to facilitate the process of learning to write fiction (Hemingway believed that it cannot be taught, only learned, and I am not about to quarrel with the man who taught twentieth-century Americans how to write their stories in their own language, not on that point, at least) is that the only way to judge whether the student is progressing is by reading what the student has written. Which means that the student cannot anticipate the course by stockpiling manuscripts written over a long preparatory period including intermittent bouts of inspiration, but must write or rewrite at least some of it during the term of the course. Bear with me for a moment here: the practical problems that students and earnest teachers of writing encounter are essentially the same as those that the solitary writer faces by himself. The techniques that seem to ameliorate difficulties encountered in seminars are adaptable for application by the lonely scribe.

I prefer my students to deliver two stories of around three thousand words each, in addition to the samples they submit to qualify for admission. I do not recommend that portions of novels in progress be substituted for those stories, although I permit it, partly because I believe it's more difficult for me and other members of the seminar to gauge the effectiveness of an episode taken from the context of the surrounding long story, and partly because I belong to the faction holding that divulging pieces of long fiction still in process can be detrimental to their prospects of completion. Presentation of a piece of a novel in class is a form of publishing, and that of course implies that the whole job has been finished. It is very difficult to tell a story twice, both times successfully. There is a wide divergence of opinion on this point, but I strongly believe that nothing should be read or shown to anyone else until the writer, always his own first reader, is either satisfied that he cannot improve it further by himself, or that he is hopelessly stuck and will never finish the story by himself— which is usually, sad to say, a dead giveaway that the story isn't working, can't be made to work, and must be binned with other false starts that seemed so promising and exciting when they were first made.

The obligation to circulate and read passes in rotation arranged to offer as much leeway as possible for each writer to weather the inevitable dry spells, without exacerbating unavoidable feelings of pressure to produce. This does not even begin to train the student how to handle the pressure he or she will feel if later fortunate enough to be blandished into trying to support a family on the full-time scribbler's wildly fluctuating earnings (well, there is one way, of course: write something that makes you so rich you can live through fallow periods on the interest money, but since I haven't figured that out myself, I don't know how to prepare anyone else to deal with it.)

Still, for all my good intentions, anxiety persists. The student feels he or she must demonstrate progress in order to gratify the sensitive ego of the designated facilitator, and the instructor, already jittery enough about tackling a job arguably impossible to do, and by profession a presumably experienced neurotic, suffers combined attacks of guilt and feelings of inadequacy. The wonder of the whole process is not that it occasionally delivers some felicitous results; it is that it does not invariably reduce all of the participants to states of gibbering idiocy and complete paralysis of the imagination.

There is no antidote for this progressive condition, and it never goes away. As Irwin Shaw mused in his introduction to his selected stories, writing is simultaneously the most fun you can legally have for an entire workday, and damned hard work. But there is an emollient of multiple ingredients for the bruises that result from what Shaw called "an intellectual contact sport, similar to football." It is necessary to remember at all times, especially when most frustrated and cranky, that *the writer is always at the mercy of his story.* Some stories are better than others. There isn't anything that any writer can do to change this. Robert Penn Warren's story based on the career of Huey Long—*All the King's Men,* 1946—was a better book than the one he did about a plantation owner's daughter sold into slavery—*Band of Angels,* 1955. This was partly because he allowed his prose to become overstuffed in the later book, but that fault I think was probably attributable to his own uneasy suspicion that his material simply wasn't exciting him as much, so he juiced up the prose to help it along. Any given writer can fool any given reader except one on any given day; the one he cannot trick is himself.

Because the writer is in a manner of speaking the victim of the story, passive in the first stage of its conception—Henry James referred to the germ of the story as the gift, or *donnée*, the structure that the writer glimpses before a mark appears on the paper—it is not only foolhardy but useless and depressing to expect that the story you write this week or this month will necessarily be superior to the one you wrote last month or last year. It is desirable to learn from your mistakes —that is why you should read your stories aloud—and to strive to improve your technique, but it is bootless to be saddened when it becomes apparent to you that while your methodology and skills have improved, the fiction that you are producing is not substantially better. I always believe that the novel I am working on is the best that I have ever done. Since I always write the next one before its predecessor is published, that being my partly superstitious protection against F. Scott Fitzgerald's dire warning and at least partial proof that there are no second acts in American lives, I am at least insincere when I assure interviewers that the new book they have in their hands is the best that I have done. But this does not mean I am necessarily wrong, or that what I have said to them is false; for all I know, it is in the objective sense absolutely true. Besides, anyone who asks a writer not only to assess the value of his own work but to rate it as well against what he or she has done before (almost never is any interviewer boorish enough to suggest that the writer evaluate his work in comparison with someone else's; when that does happen, misprision is not only allowable, but mandatory) deserves a fanciful answer.

That is why Hemingway's boastful habit of ranking himself by ranking his prowess ahead of that of writers such as Tolstoy and Turgenev—an egregious act, considering that he did not read Russian and was consequently basing his judgment on translations: what somebody else had said they had written—is not only obnoxious to the reader, but pernicious to the writer. To the reader it is mere invidious bravado, but to the writer it implies that he is not only competing against his predecessors and contemporaries, but against himself as well. When a real writer reads or hears a story, the issue is not whether he or she wrote it, or someone else did, and it is not whether it is better or not as good as any other story; it is whether the story by itself is any good. Literary *Schadenfreude*—one writer tearing down another's respectable work in the evident effort to build up his own—is evidence that that rule of professionalism has been violated. Dejection originating in the belief that what you are writing is not as good—meaning: as compelling, as important, or as thrilling; that sort of thing—as what you have written previously is evidence that you are ignoring the rule yourself, and placing yourself in hazard of creative impotence.

I think the only way to find out whether the story in your mind is any good is to sit down by yourself and try to put all of it on paper (and I think one reason why so little of the fiction that we see on television and movie screens is any good is because Hollywood's creative process usually begins with a version of the White House BOGSAT custom chronicled by Ward Just in *Jack Gance:* a Bunch Of Guys Sitting Around A Table and trying to committee stories into being). If the story interests you enough to provoke you into temporarily withdrawing from society long enough to tell it, there is at least a fair possibility that when you are finished, it will interest other people enough to prompt them to forgo companionship long enough to read it. If that proves to be the case, and one of those people is an editor, he or she may actually give you some money in order to make the opportunity available to a whole lot of other people, which is presumably what you had in mind as your ultimate objective when you began spoiling the paper.

Understand when you sit down that what you will have when you finish and get up will almost certainly not be all the story that you thought you had in mind when you started. It will certainly seem to be less than what you had in mind, because it is almost always impossible ever to capture on the page precisely the symmetrical vision that beguiled your imagination. It may in reality be very well more than your first inkling suggested, because your characters have acquired larger and more complex dimensions than the relatively vague forms you initially imagined. It is very important to allow them to do this, to take over the story to the point at which you feel more like an intelligent observer taking dictation and making notes about surroundings than a meddlesome proprietor officiously dictating the conduct of the customers in his restaurant. If you try to discipline your characters, they will become surly and clam up on you, and that will fix you good.

It is especially important to exercise strict self-restraint when writing fiction today, because we have gotten something in exchange for the right to be as prolix as our nineteenth-century professional forebears were: while their readers expected them to be judgmental and pronounce moral assessments of their characters, they also required their scribblers to be very circumspect when they related the acts on which they based those judgments. Nathaniel Hawthorne did this skillfully; the Reverend Arthur Dimmesdale's fatally consuming guilt is the consequence of his cowardly refusal to take the blame for knocking up poor Hester Prynne, but a reader would have to be most ingenious to find stimulation to sexual arousal by reading about how she earned her scarlet letter. Nearly ninety years later, Maxwell Perkins alarmed Charles Scribner by leaving on his own desk a note reminding himself to force his unbridled Thomas Wolfe to delete certain words from one of his manuscripts; the note in part read "shit, piss, fuck." When Norman Mailer and James Jones wrote about American fighting men after World War II, their hard-bitten combat troops were editorially restricted to pronouncing the Great Australian Adjective as "fug," an inelegant fake classically compromising not only the priggishness of the day but the verisimilitude of the dialogue. When John Cheever's *The Wapshot Chronicle* prompted the Book-of-the-Month Club to offer him his first chance at some real money in 1956, the selection was imperiled for a while by the club's insistence that he cut the word *fuck,* which he on principle refused to do—Cheever won. So when you write today about characters who are nice, allow them to talk and act nicely; and when you write about characters who are not so nice, write down what they say and do, to demonstrate it.

You will of course hope as you compose that your readers will not be able to avoid making their own judgments about the characters of the people that you have portrayed (though you may very well be startled by the disparity between those judgments and your own), and that they will want to do so—indeed, insist on doing it. That is a large part of their motive for reading what you have written, and they are entitled to expect that you will give them all the data, however disgraceful or distasteful, that they need to inform their verdicts.

Wherever possible—I was going to write *always* but there's no future in making rules that can't be obeyed—those data should consist of facts, not conclusions. If your character has gotten himself into a nasty and dangerous fix, and that makes him wish nostalgically he were back in a place where he was safe and happy, do not write: "Robert Jordan reckoned he was liable to get himself killed by one of these unstable and villainous illiterates unless he killed at least one of them first." Write instead that after he had been begrudged a cup of wine, he produced a flask of absinthe he had brought with him from Paris and mixed some of it with water, and that he allowed one of the dangerous men to sample it. Write, as Hemingway did in chapter four of *For Whom the Bell Tolls:*

It was a milky yellow now with water and he hoped the gypsy would not take more than a swallow. There was very little of it left and one cup of it took the place of the evening papers, of all the old evenings in cafés, of all the chestnut trees that would be in bloom now in this month, of the great slow horses of the outer boulevards, of book shops, of kiosques, and of galleries, of the Parc Montsouris, of the Stade Buffalo, and of the Butte Chaumont, of the Guaranty Trust company and the Ile de la Cité, of Foyot's old hotel, and of being able to read and relax in the evening; of all the things he had enjoyed and forgotten that came back to him when he tasted that opaque, bitter, tongue-numbing, brain-warming, stomach-warming, idea-changing liquid alchemy.

I suggest to you that it is irrelevant whether Hemingway's reader of 1940 or the reader he will acquire in 1990 and long after that as well has ever been in Paris or actually remembers any of the places Robert Jordan knew, or has ever tasted absinthe or truly likes the stuff (it pours green from the bottle, smells of the wormwood used to make it, tastes something like licorice, proofs out around 136—nearly sixty percent stronger than Johnnie Walker Red—and is rumored to rot the brain; the rumors are strong enough so that it's banned in most nations). What matters, and what makes that passage so powerfully effective, is that the reader in his mind's eye *sees* the Paris that Jordan so misses and regrets now that he has gotten himself into danger. Because the reader *sees* that Paris through Jordan's eyes, he does not need to be *told* flat out that Jordan misses it and that he wonders why he left to join the Spanish civil war, and could not in fact *be* told with anything approximating the same impact.

Hemingway could do that because he knew Paris well. The data were his own, and because they belonged to him, he could share them with his readers so successfully that those who had their own data about the city would find resonances with their own recollections and would understand at once what Hemingway was revealing about Robert Jordan's character and sensibility, *and so would readers who have never been to France,* or even wished to go there. If you want your reader to understand something about a given character, his habits of intellection and control of his emotions, show the reader what the character thinks about, and then the reader will think about it too.

There is a device that at least used to be popular among teachers of psychology, and remains instructive for writers: "For the next five minutes do not think about an orange owl." The usual, immediate effect of that instruction is of course to prompt all within earshot to try to imagine such a preposterous beast as an owl tinted orange; the secondary effect is general laughter, as everyone present for the challenge divines that everybody else is also engaged in the same silly business. The point of the exercise is supposed to be that liberal arts students do not follow directions very well, and that the power of suggestion ignites the imagination to ponder things that its possessor has never seen—the existence of which he would ordinarily, and with excellent reason, seriously doubt. That is a pretty good summary of what we writers are after when we seek to seduce the reader into that willing suspension of disbelief we need to do our jobs. If one of the surest ways of firing the imagination hot enough to melt incredulity is by focusing the reader's attention on a concrete object he can visualize, that is a method we ought to prize. And that is what Hemingway did.

So that is the other side of the coin of advice against allowing the reputations of the masters to intimidate you. While keeping in mind another F. Scott Fitzgerald maxim, that the test of a first-rate intelligence is the ability to function while simultaneously entertaining two contradictory ideas, surely the measure that every writer aspires to meet, exert yourself mightily (as Peter Rabbit did, trying to escape from Farmer McGregor; Beatrix Potter was a fine writer, not merely one who wrote stories for children, and deserves more credit than she generally gets for her accomplishments as the teller of stories that adults can read to entrance children, without contracting diabetes themselves) to perceive work that is clearly masterly, and learn everything that you possibly can from reading it. Remember what might be called the Defoe Defense: Bad writers plagiarize; good writers steal. Develop the attitude toward fiction by others that the poachers expressed when they raided the game abounding on the estates of their noble landlords: it doesn't matter if somebody else, even one of your friends, raised the succulent deer and the tasty pheasant solely for the purposes of his own shooting amusement, and the enjoyment of his social equals gathered around his table. If you're hungry to improve your technique, and there's meat to be had to nourish that appetite, take it. No matter who raised it, or what effort and expense he or she went to, to do it. Sullen envy is just as poor a substitute for food for the ravenous creative mind as it is for a fat roast in an empty belly.

5

An artist is his own fault.
–John O'Hara

John O'Hara wrote that sentence in his introduction to the Viking *Portable F. Scott Fitzgerald,* edited by Dorothy Parker and published in 1945. O'Hara admired Fitzgerald exceedingly (and, I think, excessively), managing to do this only by reminding himself regularly of the distinction between the work that captivated him and the often-insupportable behavior of the writer who produced it. O'Hara was assisted in his performance of that balancing act by his clear-eyed awareness that he himself in his time had been a devil to live with, and was therefore obliged to tolerate intractable conduct by others (persons bent upon becoming writers had done well to begin by training members of their immediate families, and their friends, to practice the same sort of tolerance, another piece of ticklish business about which I have no wisdom to offer).

"A little matter of twenty-five years ago," O'Hara wrote,

I, along with half a million other men and women between fifteen and thirty, fell in love with a book. It was the real thing, that love. As one who tries to avoid the use of simile and metaphor, I cannot refrain here from comparing my first and subsequent meetings with that book to a first and subsequent meeting with The Girl. You meet a certain girl and you say to yourself, in the words of a 1928 song, 'How long has this been going on?' The charm has to be there from the very beginning, but then you see that this time it is more than charm (although charm can be enough). The construction, of a book or a girl, has to be there from the very beginning, but then you see that this time it is more than the construction (although construction can be enough in the case of the girl).

Yes, O'Hara was a male chauvinist pig, but he was still a good writer, and that's what's important here.

Well, not to back away from the point too long or too often, I took the book to bed with me, and I still do, which is more than I can say of any girl I knew in 1920.

After the appearance of that book I was excitedly interested in almost anything written by F. Scott Fitzgerald; his novels, short stories, and his nonfiction articles. He was born in September 1896 and I got here in January 1905, both of us just for the ride, but in spite of the at that time very important difference in our ages I regarded him as one of us. He knew what we were talking about and thinking about, if you could call it thinking, and what he knew was every bit as true of us who were of Earth '05 as of the '96 codgers.

The book was *This Side of Paradise*. It was not included in this volume. Mrs. Parker did not consult me. . . .

Mrs. Parker was right, and John O'Hara's judgment at the age of forty was adversely (but quite understandably, and altogether charmingly) affected by his recollection of the magical spell cast upon him in his youth by Fitzgerald's jejeune first book—I hesitate to call it "a novel"; "a pastiche," maybe? A "collage"? It is becoming for a writer to persist into middle age in veneration of the stuff that seized his youthful mind and inspired him to mimicry, but it is stupid for later arrivals to accept his loyal pronouncements at face value.

I bring all this up for two reasons that I think are important to the developing writer. The first is that F. Scott Fitzgerald's work is vastly overrated. The second is that the work of his loyal disciple, John O'Hara, is astoundingly underrated. The result is that Americans who would like to become writers, at the shag end of the twentieth century, get hammered in schools with the mythology that Scott Fitzgerald was a great American writer of the twentieth century (O'Hara was strident in his averments that Fitzgerald merited a Pulitzer and a Nobel far more than did Pearl Buck or Sinclair Lewis, and he was right about that), and then they go and believe it.

F. Scott Fitzgerald *wrote* one novel. One. Count it. One. It was a splendid novel, *The Great Gatsby.* He *published This Side of Paradise,* which was a stinker, and *The Beautiful and Damned,* which was an even bigger stinker, and he *published Tender Is the Night,* which was a potentially good book that had a broken back (he rewrote the ending before it was reissued, and he still didn't have it right, and he knew it, and then he died), and after he was dead *they* published *The Last Tycoon,* which he hadn't even *finished,* not even once, before his heart attacked him. You can look this up. You can read *Some Sort of Epic Grandeur: The Life of F. Scott Fitzgerald,* by

Matthew J. Bruccoli (1981), or you can read *Scott Fitzgerald*, by Andrew Turnbull (1962). It's all there—Bruccoli's book has more of it because he had better access to sources.

What is all there is that Scott Fitzgerald was in fact ill-used by the fate that positioned him to become the Chronicler of the Jazz Age. After *TSOP* was published, he was rich and famous. He didn't stay rich for long, because he and his wife, Zelda Sayre, ignored the distinction between recurring income—the kind that their pals Gerald and Sara Murphy could depend upon from his inheritance of ownership in the Mark Cross leathergoods stores—and nonrecurring income, which is the kind you get when your byline is hot and the *Saturday Evening Post* is paying you between fifteen thousand and thirty thousand dollars a year in 1920s dollars, before the income tax was really humming.

He did stay famous, though, and that was bad for him too. Fame insulated him by making him into a Writer before he was twenty-five, and the money deceived him into believing he was Rich, so that the only things he really got to know were the ones he had learned before he had plenty of money and was young and handsome and in love with a girl who wouldn't marry him until he became rich and famous, and what happened to you when you were rich and famous, and then what happened to you after you had finished being rich but had not stopped being famous.

That is not enough to support a writer over the average span of life as an adult in America. John O'Hara died in 1970 at sixty-five, with a massive body of work behind him precisely because he knew a lot of stories he had learned before he became rich and famous (but not honored, with unearned degrees and prizes, and that bothered him so much he incautiously expressed his anger publicly, which of course guaranteed that what he had not received before he would not get afterward). *Appointment in Samarra* is easily the best of his novels, and you should read it, but *Ten North Frederick* and

From the Terrace, of which he was extremely proud, seem to me diffuse and poorly structured; they merit reading, and reward it generously, but they are not in my estimation good models for the aspiring novelist. I have a theory that probably stands up no better than O'Hara's most ambitious long works seem to me to do: I think writers tend to think in set lengths, so that a John Updike is most naturally comfortable with a novel's scope, and a John O'Hara was most at ease writing the short story (O'Hara predicted this would be his fate: to be known as a writer of short stories, not a novelist, and he resented that, too, but he was an ordinary novelist, and he was a superb writer of short stories, so his indignation is irrelevant). For a sampling of his stories, try any of his collections —*Assembly; The Horse Knows the Way; And Other Stories*—or my narrow favorite, *The Cape Cod Lighter,* published by Random House in 1962 (for enlightenment about the man himself, see *The O'Hara Concern,* by the ubiquitous Matthew J. Bruccoli, published in 1975). "Appearances," which follows, comes from *The Cape Cod Lighter;* I had more trouble making this selection than any other in this text, simply because there are so many wonderful O'Hara stories from which to choose (he published 374 of them), and at least three dozen are in the first rank of twentieth-century American fiction. But anyway, here it is.

Howard Ambrie stopped the car at the porte-cochere to let his wife out, then proceeded to the garage. The M-G was already there, the left-hand door was open, and the overhead lamp was burning, indicating that their daughter was home. Ambrie put the sedan in its customary place, snapped out the light, rang down the door, and walked slowly toward the house. He stopped midway and looked at the sky. The moon was high and plain, the stars were abundant.

In the kitchen his wife had poured him a glass of milk, which rested on the table with a piece of sponge cake. "I'll be able to play tomorrow after all," said Howard Ambrie. "There's hardly a cloud in the sky."

"Oh, then you've thought it over," said Lois Ambrie.

"Thought what over?"

"Jack Hill's funeral. You're not going."

"Was I thinking it over?"

"You said at dinner that you hadn't decided whether to go or not," said Lois Ambrie.

"That was only because I knew the McIvers planned to go."

"I don't understand your reasoning," she said.

"Well, then I'll explain it to you. Peter and Cathy *want* to go to the funeral. I don't. No reason why I should. But I didn't want to inflict my *not* wanting to go on their *wanting* to go. Impose, I guess, would be a better word. Influence them. Or for that matter, take away their pleasure in going to the service. I said I hadn't made up my mind, and so there was no discussion about it. If I'd said I definitely wasn't going, or if I'd definitely said I wasn't going, they would have wanted to know why."

"What would you have told them?"

"What would I have told them? I'd have told them that I'd much rather play golf tomorrow."

"Well, that would have started a discussion, all right," she said.

"I know it would," he said. "And I know what the discussion would have been. Wasn't Jack Hill one of my best friends? Couldn't I play golf after the service? And so forth. But I disposed of all that by simply saying I hadn't made up my mind."

"You disposed of it as far as the McIvers were concerned, but will you tell *me* why you're not going?"

"I don't mind telling you. In the first place, I've never considered Jack Hill one of my best friends. He wasn't. He was a lifelong acquaintance, a contemporary, our families were always friends, or friendly. And if you wanted to stretch a point, we were related. All of which you know. But in a town this size, at least until just before the War, damn near everybody is related in some way or other."

"Yes, and damn near everybody will be at that funeral tomorrow," she said. "Therefore your absence will be noticed."

"Maybe it will. I thought of that. But the fact is, I never liked Jack and he never liked me. If the circumstances were reversed, I'm sure he'd be playing golf tomorrow. There won't be many more days we can play this year. I noticed driving by this afternoon, they've taken the pins out of the cups, and I wouldn't be surprised if they filled in the holes. The golf shop is boarded up for the winter. In fact, Charley closed up a week ago and went to Florida. I hope there's enough hot water for a shower. I hate to come in after playing golf in this weather and find no hot water."

"You're playing in the morning," she said.

"Playing in the morning. We're meeting at ten o'clock, playing eighteen holes. Having something to eat. Probably the usual club sandwiches. And then playing bridge. I'll be home around five, I should think."

"Who are you playing with?"

"Same three I play with every Saturday, and they won't be missed at Jack's funeral."

"No, they certainly won't be. None of Jack's old friends, and none of your old friends, either, not in that foursome."

"Lois, you talk as though the whole of Suffolk County were going to be at the church tomorrow, checking to see who stayed away. Are *you* going to the funeral?"

"Yes, I'm going. Or I was. I don't know whether I want to go without you."

"Oh, hell, call up somebody and go with *them.*"

"No, if you're not going, I won't. That would make your not going so much more noticeable. 'Where's Howard?' 'Playing golf.'"

"Listen, I'm not going, so don't try to persuade me."

"I think you ought to go," she said.

"No."

"I'll make one more try. I'm *asking* you to go," she said.

"And my answer is I think you're being God damn unreasonable about this. Jack Hill and I have known each other over fifty years, we were thrown together by age and financial circumstances. His family and my family had about the same amount of dough. But when we got older and could choose our friends, he never chose me and I never chose him. We were never enemies, but maybe if we had been we'd have found out why we didn't like each other. Then maybe we could have been friends. But we never had any serious quarrel. We never had a God damn thing."

"He was an usher at our wedding."

"I *knew* you'd bring that up. That was twenty-five years ago, and I had to have him and he had to have me because our parents were friends. It was one of those automatic things in a small town. I couldn't ask one of the clammers, and he couldn't ask one of the potato farmers, but that's *all* it was. And since you bring that up, about being ushers, Celia didn't ask me to be a pallbearer or whatever the hell she's having. Celia has more sense about this than you have."

"There aren't going to be any pallbearers, and you know it."

"All right, I do know it. And she's very sensible, Celia."

"I'm asking you again. Howard, please. Put off your golf till after lunch, and go to this funeral with me. It isn't much to ask."

"Why do you care so much whether I go or not?"

"Because I don't want Celia knowing that you stayed away."

"Oh, Christ. All right. Although why you care what Celia knows or doesn't know—you and Celia were never that good friends."

"But you will go?"

"Yes. I said I would, and I will. But you certainly screwed up my weekend."

"You can play in the afternoon and Sunday."

"Father O'Sullivan can't play Saturday afternoon, he has to hear confessions, and he can't play Sunday at all. And Joe Bushmill is going skeet-shooting this Sunday. It's not only my schedule you loused up."

"I'm sorry about that, Howard, but I do appreciate it."

"Oh, sure. You have no idea how you complicate things. We had to get a fourth for bridge, because O'Sullivan has to be in church at three o'clock. And now they'll have to get someone to take my place at golf *and* bridge."

"I'll do something for you sometime."

"Why didn't you make your big pitch before tonight?"

"Because I took for granted that you'd be going to the funeral. I just took it for granted."

"I suppose the same way that people took for granted that Jack Hill was a friend of mine. Well, he wasn't. I'm going to bed. Oh, Amy's home. The M-G's in the garage."

"I know. Goodnight, dear."

"Goodnight," he said. He bent down and kissed her cheek.

Light showed on the floor beneath Amy's bedroom door, and he knocked gently. "Amy? You awake?" he said softly.

"Father? Come in."

She was sitting up in bed, and when he entered she took off her reading glasses. "Hi," she said.

"What are you reading?" he said.

"Detective story. Who won?"

"Oh, your mother and I took them. We always do, at their house, and they usually win when they come here." He sat on the chaise-longue. "As Mr. McCaffery says, what kind of a day's it been today?"

"Fridays are always easier than other days. The children seem to behave better on Friday. That is, their behavior is better, probably because they're in a better mood. Their schoolwork isn't as good, but you can't have everything."

"Do you like teaching?"

"Not very much, but I like the children."

"Well, it's nice having you home for a year."

"Thank you, Father. It's nice being home."

"Is it?" he said.

"Have a cigarette?" She held up a package.

"No thanks. You didn't answer my question."

"I know I didn't. Yes, it's nice being home."

"But that's as far as you'll commit yourself?" he said.

"That's as far as I want to commit myself."

"You mean you don't want to think more deeply than that?"

"Yes, I guess that's what I mean. I'm comfortable here, I have my job, my car to run around in, and I had no idea we had so many detective stories. This one was copyrighted 1924."

"There are some older than that, early Mary Roberts Rinehart," he said. "Believe I will have one of your cigarettes." He caught the pack she tossed him and lit a cigarette. "Are you making any plans for next year?"

"Not exactly. I may get married again. I may not."

"This time you ought to have children right away."

"It wouldn't be so good if I had a child now, would it?"

"It might have kept you together, Amy, a child. We had you the first year, your mother and I."

"Father, you're practically implying that if you hadn't had me—"

"I know what I'm implying," he said. "And I know you're no fool. You know it's often been touch and go with your mother and I. You've seen that."

"I guess it is with everybody. But a child wouldn't have kept Dave and me together. Nothing would."

"Well, what really separated you?"

"Well, it wasn't his fault. I fell in love with someone else."

"The man you're thinking of marrying?"

"No."

"The man you're thinking of marrying is that doctor in Greenport?"

"Yes."

"But the man you left Dave for was someone else?"

"Yes."

"And what's happened to him? He's gone out of your life?"

She looked at him sharply. "Yes."

"Why? Was he married?"

"Yes."

"Where did you know him? At Cornell?"

"No, Father. And don't ask me any more questions, please. You voluntarily said you wouldn't ask me any questions, you promised that when I came home after my divorce."

"I did, but with the understanding that when you were ready to tell us, you would. It isn't just idle curiosity, Amy. Your mother and I have a right to know those things, if only to keep you from making the same mistakes all over again."

"I won't make that mistake over again. And I'm not ready to tell you what happened to me with Dave."

"As far as I know, Dave was a hell of a nice boy."

"He was, and is, but I wasn't a hell of a nice girl. No father likes to face that fact about his daughter, but there it is."

"You're not a tart, you're not a chippy."

"No. But that's not all there is besides virgins, Father."

"Oh, I know that."

"Well, when does a girl get to be a tart in your estimation? Is it a question of how many men she sleeps with?"

"It most certainly is, yes."

"How many?"

"Yes, I walked into that one, didn't I? Well, a girl who sleeps with more than two men before she gets married, she's on her way. I can see a girl having an affair the first time she thinks she's in love. And then the second time, when she's more apt to be really in love. But the next time she'd better be damned sure; or she's going to be a pushover for everybody."

"Well—that's more or less my record. The second time was also the man I left Dave for."

"Oh, you had an affair and married Dave and continued to have this other affair?"

"Yes."

"What's going to prevent your having an affair with this same guy after you marry your doctor? . . . You had an affair with a married man before you married Dave. He sounds like a real son of a bitch."

"I guess maybe he was, although I didn't think so. I guess he was, though."

"You're not still seeing him?"

"No. I did after I divorced Dave, but not after I began dating the doctor."

"You're—to use an old-fashioned word—faithful to the doctor?"

"Oh, you're so smart, Father. You've tricked me into admitting I'm having an affair with the doctor. The answer is yes."

"Hell, I knew you were probably having an affair with the doctor. I'm no fool, either, you know. Well, it's been a very interesting conversation between father and daughter. It's a good thing I'm not *my* father, or you'd be—well, you wouldn't be here."

"No, but we wouldn't have had this conversation, either."

"You have a point. Goodnight, dear." He kissed her cheek and she squeezed his hand. "There *is* that," he said. "We wouldn't have had this conversation. Goodnight again."

"Goodnight, Father," she said.

The girl sat in her bed, holding her glasses loosely with her right hand, her book with her left, both hands lying on the pink comforter. Her mother came in. "What was that all about?" said Lois Ambrie.

"Our conversation? Oh, mostly about Dave and me."

"He didn't say anything about Jack Hill?"

"No."

"I'll be glad when Jack is buried and out of the way."

"I know," said Amy.

"Your father is getting closer to the truth, Amy."

"I guess he is."

"I had a very difficult time persuading him to go to the funeral tomorrow."

"Why did you bother?"

"Appearances. 'Why didn't Howard Ambrie go to Jack Hill's funeral?' They'd be talking about that for a month, and somebody'd be sure to say something to Celia. And then Celia'd start asking herself questions."

"I wonder. I think Mrs. Hill stopped asking questions a long time ago. She should have. I wasn't the only one he played around with."

"You can be so casual about it. 'Played around with.' And you haven't shown the slightest feeling about him, his dying."

"I didn't show any because I haven't got any. Other than relief. I'm not grief-stricken that he died, Mother. As long as he was alive I was afraid to marry Joe. Now I think I can marry Joe and settle down in Greenport and be what I always wanted to be. But not while Jack was alive. That's the effect he had on me."

"He was no good," said Lois Ambrie. "Strange how your father knew that without knowing why."

"I know why," said Amy. "Jack was the kind of man that husbands are naturally suspicious of. Father was afraid Jack would make a play for you. Instead he made a play for me, but Father never gave that a thought."

"I suppose so. And in your father's eyes it would be just as bad for me to cover up for you as it would have been for me to have had an affair with Jack. I'll be glad when he's out of the way. Really glad when you can marry Joe."

"Did you go over and call on Mrs. Hill?"

"I went over this afternoon, but she wasn't seeing anyone. Fortunately."

"She *is* grief-stricken?"

"I don't think it's that. No, I don't think it's that. As you said a moment ago, Celia probably stopped asking questions a long time ago. I'd put it another way. That she's known for years about Jack. Now she doesn't want to see anybody because whatever she's feeling, she doesn't want anybody to see *her*. Grief, or relief. Maybe she doesn't even know yet what she feels. Fear, maybe. Whatever he was, she stuck with him all those years, and suddenly he's gone and she's fifty-two or -three. I don't know what's in Celia's mind, but I'm glad I'm not her. Did you see Joe tonight?"

"Yes, I had dinner with him. We had dinner at his sister's house in Southold. Spaghetti. She's a very good cook."

"That will be quite something, an Ambrie marrying an Italian boy. Will you have to turn Catholic?"

"I will if he wants me to. If it means that much to him. I'm not sure it does, but it would probably make a difference to his family."

"Can he marry a divorced woman? I have no idea what the Catholic church says on that."

"We haven't discussed it, so I don't know either."

"Your father's great friends with the new Catholic priest, O'Sullivan. They play golf and bridge together every Saturday."

"So I gather. When the time comes, whatever they say I'll do."

"It would be quite a feather in their cap, an Ambrie turning Catholic."

"They may not see it that way. I understand they can be very tough about some things."

"Well, I suppose it's their turn. Goodness knows I still can't get used to the idea of having one in the White House. Can I get you a glass of milk or anything?"

"No thanks, Mother."

"Then I guess I'll be off to bed."

"Mother?"

"What?"

"I'm sorry I caused you and Father so much trouble. You especially. All those lies you had to tell."

"Oh, that's all right. It's over now. And it was really harder on your father. He never knew why he didn't like that man."

"And *you* couldn't tell him, *could* you, Mother?"

"What?"

"Oh, Mother."

Lois Ambrie looked at her daughter. "Is that another detective story you're reading? You mustn't get carried away, Amy." She smiled. "Goodnight, dear," she said, and closed the door.

There is a whole set of reasons why "Appearances" works so well, and those reasons deserve some individual reflection by the scribbler aspiring to accomplish as much with his 3,300 words or so as O'Hara did with his. And don't succumb here to the misapprehension that what makes a story work is information irrelevant to the would-be writer of novels; the same rules not only apply to the construction of novels, but are even more important.

The first O'Hara characteristic that almost invariably distinguishes his work is *the density of his material.* Consider what he accomplishes in the eight lines of his first paragraph. He has informed us that Howard Ambrie and his wife are sufficiently well-off to live in a house with a porte cochere, which the dictionary defines as a structure at the entrance of a building, designed to shelter passengers arriving in carriages. Plainly Mr. Ambrie and his wife are not riffraff, but a couple of some wealth and social standing.

Since Mr. and Mrs. Ambrie have been out together in the same car, and the MG has returned since they departed, we know that there is someone most likely younger than they who is living in their comfortable house. MG (for Morris Garage) probably doesn't deliver to readers of the last decade of the twentieth century the same flash of recognition that it offered to readers in the early sixties, when O'Hara published

The Cape Cod Lighter, because MG was later ingested by British Leyland, an ungainly corporate conglomerate that mismanaged the manufacturer of those sporty, buzzing, neat little roadsters right out of existence, so the only time you see an MG now in any sort of decent shape is when you attend a *concours d'élégance*, where a lot of old goats in tweed jackets and camel-hair berets stand around under striped awnings and try to restore their lost youth with very cold martinis and the consoling sight of all those nifty two-seaters toothbrushed into something close to the pristine state they had when they were new, thirty years and more ago. But when O'Hara used that little car as a code, and then beautifully specified that its operator was not only the raffish sort of devil who would want such a car, but probably also a careless one as well (the driver's-side door had been left open, and the overhead garage light not shut off), he communicated all of this at once: Howard Ambrie's daughter was home and her attitude toward cars and money irritated her father. O'Hara confirms this by reporting that Howard walked slowly toward the house and paused en route to ponder the heavens, meaning: he took a little time to calm down and think—and I have just used about three hundred words to deliver what O'Hara communicated in about eighty.

That is what I mean by *the density of his material*. When John O'Hara described physical objects, he did so with two objectives in mind. The first was to enable the reader to picture the character in his own imagination (and note here that O'Hara provided no details whatsoever about Howard Ambrie's physique, attire, haircut, body temperature, or color of eyes, and also that he scorned to *tell* us either that Ambrie was bothered by something that somehow involved his daughter, or what that something might be; that is because Ambrie's physical stature and wardrobe had no bearing on the story, and because the whole purpose of the story was to *show* us that Ambrie is upset, and allow us to figure out the reasons).

O'Hara's second purpose in packing his narrative to such high specific gravity was the same as the coach's purpose in requiring that his athletes perform calisthenics before beginning actual competition: to warm up the muscles the game will test. *Reading is not a spectator sport, not when the writing is done by a John O'Hara; it is a participatory event,* just as his disciple, Irwin Shaw, suggested with his metaphor comparing its creation to a football game, and the reason it is so captivating is because it gives the mind such good, brisk exercise.

The story from the point at which Ambrie enters the house right through to the end is almost entirely dialogue. That is where the exercise and the reading enjoyment come in, and therefore the ambitious writer needs to understand not only what O'Hara was up to, but how he brought it off.

It is not some kind of a stunt. I use a lot of dialogue to tell my own stories, for reasons I will get to, and when my work, two years after O'Hara died in 1970, began to get some attention, I received the same kind of accolades for writing dialogue (though, I am sure, nowhere near as many) as were accorded him. And, perhaps somewhat sooner than he did, I became very weary in the face of them. This is partly because I was aware that O'Hara's proficiency with dialogue had been paradoxically invoked as grounds to dismiss his work, and I knew that was wrong, and partly because it was being used to disparage mine, which I resented just as thoroughly as he did when it was his.

The substance of the nastier dismissal notes in my case was that it was to be expected that the hoods and thugs and lawyers who populated my first book, *The Friends of Eddie Coyle,* were of course authentic portrayals, because, after all, I had been an assistant attorney general in the Organized Crime Section of the Massachusetts Department of the Attorney

General, and then an assistant U.S. attorney in Boston. So far, so good—no quarrel with that. I did in those positions supplement my store of data about how the Mob works, adding to the base I had laid down as a reporter for the Providence *Journal* and the Associated Press. I didn't copy any of my characters from life, but the characters I wrote about did things that real hard guys had done, and refrained scrupulously from doing things that real hard guys would never do.

But there followed from that premise a leap of logic so breathtaking as to reduce this helpless onlooker to near-speechless anger. The explanation proposed for the ability of my wicked characters to portray themselves so accurately almost entirely through their dialogue was that I had shamelessly pilfered their discourse entirely from transcripts of wiretaps and grand jury hearings.

It is impossible to make that preposterous deduction if you have ever taken the trouble to read even ten pages of such transcripts. Transcripts make excruciating reading, and the suffering increases in direct proportion but geometrical progression to one's own efforts to cultivate good habits of speech, and the extent of one's personal participation in the recorded discourse. Whether the speakers talk in relaxed but misguided belief that their words are not being overheard, or deliver their utterances in the uncomfortable awareness that everything they say is not only being taken down but may be used in evidence against them, they stammer, elide words, leave out prepositions, omit transition sentences, dangle participles, leave infinitives not only split but drawn and quartered on the highway, and generally trample upon all the rules of syntax. The transcripts of conversations held in either set of circumstances are of use to the aspiring writer only for their demonstration that almost nobody except the very best of public speakers can tell a story orally without a script, and those who can have memorized a script before they start.

So, once you have read enough transcripts to realize that most of those talking in front of grand juries don't want to tell the real story (while fearing prosecution for concealing it perjuriously, if they get caught), and that those whose words are intercepted are incapable of telling a story coherently, even though they sometimes wish to, you have acquired most of the profit offered by the enterprise to the aspiring scribbler. The rest is the understanding first that you will have to make it up yourself, and second that it will ring true only if the diction displays the kind of syntactical breakdowns that occur in actual speech (but rigorously limits their frequency, in order not to drive your reader nuts), while somehow advancing that same reader's understanding of the characters who are speaking, and the story they actually may not understand themselves, and almost certainly wish on no account to tell. If there is to be a story, you must write it down.

O'Hara had quite a lot to say on that point in three lectures he delivered at Rider College at Lawrenceville, New Jersey, near his home in Princeton, in 1959 and 1961 (not published until Matthew J. Bruccoli collected them and other O'Hara materials in *John O'Hara on Writers and Writing: "An Artist Is His Own Fault,"* 1977), and I think his comments are helpful here to understanding his methods in such work as "Appearances."

I have been told often enough that I write the best dialog [O'Hara preferred the spelling omitting *-ue,* so we will honor that preference in quoting him] that is being written. I make this immodest statement because many of my critics seem to feel that they have to say, or strongly imply, that my gift for dialog is all I have; or that writing dialog is not the most important attribute a novelist can have. Well, it is *not* the most essential part of an author's equipment. The basic, indispensable attribute of a novelist is the understanding of character and the ability to create characters, and they go together, since understanding without creation means no novel and no novelist. But I discovered when I was very young, before I was in my teens, that nothing could so quickly cast doubt on, and even destroy, an author's characters as bad dialog. If the people did not talk right, they were not real people. The closer to real talk, the closer to real people. . . .

A man or woman who does not write good dialog is not a first-rate writer.

I do not believe that a writer who neglects or has not learned to write good dialog can be depended upon for accuracy in his understanding of character and his creation of characters. Therefore to dismiss good dialog so lightly is evidence of a critic's incomplete understanding of what constitutes a good novel. I think I was the first to use the expression, a tin ear, in connection with the writing of bad dialog. The tin ear has always meant the inability to carry a tune, but an author who has a tin ear is one who forces his characters to say things they would not say, in ways they would not say it; and most authors have tin ears. This would not be so bad if it was an isolated fault, but it seldom is. Let me give you an example.

Some years ago, when I was writing a great many short stories for a magazine, I was called in by an editor to discuss a story in which one of the characters was an upper-class New York girl, a Spence-Chapin-Brearley type girl. I had given this girl a line of dialog which went something like this: "Robert didn't come with she and I." I repeat the line: "Robert didn't come with she and I." Now obviously the girl should have said "with her and me." The preposition *with* governing the objective case. The editor, a college graduate and a Junior League type herself, maintained that the girl would not have made the grammatical mistake I had her make. But the editor was an editor and not an author, and she had never written any dialog. She was also, let's face it, a bit of a snob, and she was trying to tell me that people like her did not make such mistakes. My point, however, was that just such a mistake was made all the time, *and that it revealed more about the girl than a hundred words of descriptive matter* [emphasis added]. Girls who went to fashionable schools would not say, "Josephine is prettier then me." They would have had it drummed into them that the verb *to be* takes the same case after it as before it, and they would go through life correctly saying, "Josephine is prettier than I." But while learning that one rule they also were developing what might be called an elegant resistance of the objective pronouns. I therefore stubbornly refused to make the change that the editor suggested, and the story appeared as I had written it. The incident had a happy ending. A few weeks later I saw the editor again and she said to me: "You were right about *she and I*. They say it all the time. Even my niece says it." Well, I knew that, or I wouldn't have written *she and I*, but I was pleased that I had been able to teach an editor to listen for the peculiarities of speech that occur in all classes.

O'Hara recalled that his debut had brought him the accusation of "having a phonographic ear. Nowadays they say a tape-recorder ear. This is supposed to be complimentary, that the author writes such good dialog that he is suspected of getting help from the magic world of electronics. I have no way of estimating how much harm that cliché may have done to young writers, not to mention how much money their poor fathers may have spent in actual purchase of tape recording apparatus. A writer, young or old, who must depend on tape recording to catch real speech had better stop wasting his time and the old man's money, while there is still hope that he can find some useful occupation. The writing of dialog," he wrote (and it gets a little ominous here, for people who are trying to learn how to write, as well as for people who are trying to help them to learn how to write, but bear up under the assault, because I think O'Hara in this respect was overly pessimistic, much as he was overly humble in the contemplation of Scott Fitzgerald's work, and I have something to say on this

113

score myself), "really cannot be learned and cannot be taught. You either have the gift or you don't. If you have the gift, you can refine it and improve on it and learn to handle it, but the absence of it is like tone deafness or the inability to mimic people."

What I have to say on that score was that O'Hara in the very same lecture partially discredited that threatening statement he had just made. He is right that no one can teach another person to write dialogue. But he contradicted his second, implied, premise, that no one can learn how to write dialogue, making it clear that the propaganda about a "gift" was mere attractive self-effacement rather slighting a considerable amount of damned hard work that he had done himself. That work had enabled him to learn how to write dialogue. Just as mine did for me.

"If you are interested in tape-recorded dialogue, which is a good study for a writer or any nonwriter who would care to read pure speech, pure in the sense that it is put down exactly as spoken, I suggest you look in your New York newspapers any Thursday morning, and read the transcripts of the day before; or, if you want to go to a little more trouble, get the transcripts of any court trials here in Trenton." The passing of the thirty years that have elapsed since O'Hara drafted that passage require a word of elaboration here for the benefit of those who had not been born, or who had been but have since forgotten Dwight D. Eisenhower's two terms as president of the United States. Ike, in office when O'Hara was lecturing at Rider, was famous for his mangled syntax; *The New York Times* and the New York *Herald Tribune* gleefully printed his Wednesday press conference remarks *verbatim*. It was nearly impossible to figure out what the hell the man was talking about, or what he actually thought about the subject under discussion. It was not until much later, long after Ike's successor, the gracefully articulate John F. Kennedy, had pirouetted his elegant way through confrontation after

114

confrontation without always communicating the full truth himself, that more reflective journalists—Nat Hentoff led the way—began to wonder whether Eisenhower's willingness to tolerate being made an illiterate figure of fun by mischievous reporters and editors had not enabled him to mask his intentions, deflecting rude or unwelcome inquiries—meaning that he was not dumb at all, but pretty deviously smart. Ike, after all, never had to take public heat for planning the Bay of Pigs invasion that Kennedy found so far advanced upon assuming office that he let the thing proceed; when Premier Castro's troops repulsed the pitiable counter-revolutionary forces attacking out of Florida, it was Kennedy who took the blame. So that is what O'Hara had in mind there, and why he had it; when he spoke at Rider, we had not caught on to Ike, and neither had O'Hara.

But O'Hara did have a good grasp of the nature of his own work, however imperfect his insight into Eisenhower's scheming. Those who studied transcripts, he predicted,

will then begin to understand why I say that I keep my dialog always under control. You will learn, for instance, that in ordinary conversation practically no one ever finishes a sentence. This is not the fault of the interrupters. It is chronic with nearly everybody. As a young newspaper reporter I discovered this great truth, simply by taking notes. I knew shorthand, because I was too young to go away to school when I finished eighth grade, and so I was kept home and took the commercial course, the only course available in parochial school in those days. I never made much use of my shorthand, except now and then to take down the speech of some brilliant orator for my own amusement. If I had quoted him verbatim he would have sued the paper. Quote any man verbatim for five minutes of extemporaneous speech and you will let him make an ass of himself. If you have absolute faith in the system of trial by jury, don't read any court transcripts. You will be terribly disillusioned to find that what the lawyers have said during a trial makes no sense when it is reduced to the printed word, and even in capital cases the judge's charge to the jury is in all probability so much gibberish. As for social conversation, if you do happen to have a tape recorder, you can embarrass yourself and your friends by playing back the recording of the most serious discussions. *It is simply amazing to find how little communication depends on things we actually say* [emphasis added].

I would phrase that a little differently. Most communication depends upon our ability to understand what is actually meant by the things that are actually said. What is said is usually a deliberate substitution for what is actually meant. This is especially so when the talker is under some kind of stress, and is fighting it while at the same time trying to conceal it.

In life, when experience has taught us that a given individual invariably misrepresents his intentions, or denies what we know to be the truth, we usually call him a liar and thereafter refuse to accept his statements, except as further proof that he is not to be trusted. This is another way of saying that he is not very good at concealing what he really means by saying something else, and that the subject on which he most grievously failed us in such an effort was one of considerable importance, so that the misrepresentation or evasion caused us harm.

On topics of lesser importance, we deceitfully submit to deceit every day, the speaker pretending to speak the truth, the listener pretending to believe what he hears. If I invite you to dinner, and you would rather stick needles in your eyes than spend ten minutes in my company, let alone an hour at the evening meal—and if we are both reasonably civilized persons with some capacity to inflict serious harm upon each

116

other, given adequate provocation—you will not respond to my invitation by replying that you think I am a rotten son of a bitch and you cannot understand how I could be so stupid as to have failed to infer that. Instead you will tell me you are very sorry, but Wednesday evening happens to be your regular bowling night, and the other members of the league would be devastated if you failed to appear. And I, being equally well brought up, will purport to accept this manifestly specious regret, and will not only suppress a sigh of relief but refrain from expressing my gratitude that I need no longer perform duets of social affection with you, whom I have always considered a silly twerp, and from then on we will be the most cordial if distant of acquaintances. We are social animals, and we have to live together in degrees of proximity that vary according to our relationships. Most of us dislike conflict unless it is clearly necessary. Harmony is essential, so we collude in as much outright prevarication and tacit concealment as may seem necessary to avoid confrontations that we do not wish to have.

Usually the desire to avoid conflict intensifies according to the particular significance of the relationship in our lives. The advice columns in the newspapers are filled with "street-angel, house-devil" complaints prompted by the behavior of loutish individuals who treat all outside their family circles with utmost consideration—i.e., they exert themselves in public to appear to be considerate, thoughtful persons, becoming so exhausted in these efforts as to be unable when at home to camouflage their vicious characters. The writers of these plaints do not understand the situation. The person who seems kind and thoughtful outside the home, and a fierce bastard inside it, cares what is thought of him or her outside the home, usually because he or she believes that those who think it can take revenge. But he or she is not afraid of family members, and therefore does not care what they think. Further, the people one encounters in ordinary commerce do not mind as much if some business acquaintance is faking good nature, even if they know it; the important thing is that the transaction be completed, and if it is, well, fine. Family members have more invested. It is usually emotional, and it's pretty difficult to place that kind of an investment somewhere else. And they have more opportunities to conduct surveillance, so it's much harder to blow smoke at them and get away with it.

It follows that the greater the emotional propinquity of the parties, the higher will be the intensity of their dependence, one upon the other, and the greater the passion provoked by one's perception that the other has betrayed him or her. Sexual arrangements are traditionally deemed the most potentially violent; the reason for this, as it is for most traditions, is that throughout history they have proven so. That is why juries and judges discriminate, even when the criminal statutes (rarely) do not, between so-called crimes of passion that result in homicides, and homicides involving strangers and based upon the hope of mere monetary gain. But other relationships of long standing—parent-child, business partner, personal friendship—also involve the threat of such dark forces being loosed by the discovery of treachery, so while the passion is less intense, it is still there, in varying amounts.

Passion is the undercurrent of the stream that nourishes the writer's art, because the possibility of its eruption inexorably creates dramatic tension. And that brings us back to "Appearances," and what John O'Hara did in it with dialogue. These are the important things we learn about Howard, Lois, and Amy Ambrie, and also about the late Jack Hill:

—Howard, an avid golfer and capable bridge player, has at least one good reason for not intending to be present at Jack Hill's funeral, *and he is not about to tell either his wife or his daughter what it is*. It is perfectly obvious that his citation of promising weather for golf on the day of Jack's interment is not that reason, as obvious to Lois as it is to us.

—Lois is unwilling to press Howard to divulge his real reason or reasons, even though she is anxiously aware that his absence from the funeral will cause gossip. She could not be aware of that certainty unless she knew what Howard's motive or motives are, and consequently could foretell the nature of the speculation guaranteed to arise after he acts on them. Therefore, Lois, grilling Howard, is really trying to make him utter his reason or reasons. She is baiting him with the purpose of forcing him either to humiliate himself in his own house, or to humiliate himself before the community by attending Jack Hill's funeral. Her selfish, explicit argument is that *she* will be embarrassed unless he embarrasses himself. This gets her nowhere; Howard is too many for her, and persists in his refusal to do either. Plainly, whatever Howard's reason or reasons are, they are enough in his eyes to warrant his judgment that her embarrassment, if he does not go to the funeral, will either be less than his own would be, if he went, or else that she deserves it. But he has a weakness, and Lois taps it: when she at last debases herself, by begging, he agrees to attend the funeral after all, for appearances.

—Amy moved back home when her marriage broke up. She makes no pretense of having been faithful to her first husband, and while she demurs to Howard's suggestion that a pregnancy might have saved her marriage, evinces no surprise when he implies that something went badly wrong in the first years of his marriage to Lois, and the only thing that saved it was the presence of Amy. The dialogue doesn't make it conclusively clear, but in the context of the discussion between Amy and her father about the effects of infidelity on a marriage, it seems reasonably arguable that either Howard or Lois had a fling after Amy was born, and at least considered ending the marriage, on more than one occasion. Much clearer is the thrust of Howard's interrogation: either he knows the identity of the man who lured Amy out of her marriage, and is daring her to say it, or he merely suspects that identity and is trying to trick her into saying it. Amy is too many for Howard, and evades his questioning.

That brings us to the conversation between Amy and Lois, after Howard has gone to bed. The girl talk is a good deal more revelatory than the husband-wife or father-daughter talk that preceded it. Lois knows that Amy's *amour impropre* was Jack Hill, and that Howard's "getting closer to the truth, Amy."

The truth of course is that Jack Hill was Amy's lover, and Howard despised him for that. This makes a nice, symmetrical, ordinary story—or it would, if O'Hara had not been such a crafty writer.

"He [Jack Hill] was no good," said Lois Ambrie. "Strange how your father knew that without knowing why."

"I know why," said Amy. "Jack was the kind of man that husbands are naturally suspicious of. Father was afraid Jack would make a play for you. Instead he made a play for me, but Father never gave that a thought."

"I suppose so. And in your father's eyes it would be just as bad for me to cover up for you as it would have been for me to have had an affair with Jack. . . ."

Which, of course, we now know Lois did. And Howard did give it a thought. Which in turn raises the lovely question What does Howard really know? And who, in this genteel family, is really the most vengeful, and therefore the most morally culpable, of Jack Hill's polite victims?

My choice is Lois; she not only made her husband a cuckold, but connived in her daughter's subsequent seduction by the very same varmint. But a good case could be made against either Howard or Amy: he for tormenting his womenfolk by making veiled references designed to keep them constantly on the edge of fear of public humiliation, while lacking the guts to confront either them or Jack Hill directly; Amy for teasing him with his private humiliation, and not omitting as well to taunt her mother with Lois's guilty motive for concealing Amy's adventure with Lois's old boyfriend.

That is what makes reading O'Hara such fun. "This theory of mine," he told his Rider College audience, "that I could be persuaded to call O'Hara's Law, that an author who does not write good dialog is not a first-rate author—is not something I stumbled on, or arrived at overnight." No, he didn't. He came by it honest, as we say, and when he obeyed O'Hara's Law we have no trouble believing what he wrote, or his candid admission: "I discovered O'Hara's Law in my own laboratory. I love to write." And he knew something else, too: all fiction is gossip, and the best of it is collected by eavesdropping.

6

I may be a rogue, but I'm a lovable rogue.
–John Forbes Thompson, Speaker, Massachusetts
House of Representatives

He stood over six feet tall. He would have been a good model for those little pen-and-ink drawings that lexicographers employ to illustrate definitions that evidently seem inadequate even to them; his portrait should have appeared next to the definition of *burly*. He was indeed a rogue, and a scoundrel to boot (when he died of acute alcoholic toxemia, in 1966, at the age of forty-four, he was under indictment for just about every variety of prohibited corruption recognized by the Commonwealth of Massachusetts); he was also a decorated veteran of World War II, commissioned on the battlefield in Normandy as a lieutenant, and when I met him for the first and only time, in 1963, he still carried with him shards of shrapnel in his legs that he could cause to grind audibly, to impress a young reporter.

The commonplace has it that newspaper people have great jobs because they meet such interesting people, and it is true. It is not true every day, when you are dealing with some carper whose garden club, school committee meeting, or Sabbath sermon did not get the play that its proprietor thought it merited, but it is true often enough so that you are never sure at the beginning of each day—or night, if you are on the lobster shift—that you will not find yourself forcefully bumped up against a fascinating person before you go off duty. Newspapering is not by any means the only line of work that carries such possibilities, but it includes a lot of them, and when you are twenty-three, with intentions of becoming a novelist, you disregard them at your peril.

I bring all of this up because I made the acquaintance of John Forbes Thompson assured that I was not going to like him. The Massachusetts Crime Commission and various grand juries had not finished with him yet, but his reputation was decidedly aromatic. Odoriferous, even. Furthermore, he had displayed *lèse majesté* toward the liberal wing of the state's Democratic party, led by Governor Endicott "Chub" Peabody, and in those days I knew who the villain of the story had to be.

It is agreeable to be in your early twenties, and know where you stand. Having had more than enough of the scut work— the aforementioned garden clubs, school committees, and impassioned sermons—that the newspaper business has always allocated to its rookies (for the excellent reason that the members of those outfits are not only the ones who buy the paper, but have the wherewithal to buy the goods advertised therein—dull to write and dull to read, but boy, that stuff sells papers, and that's what pays the salaries of the novices), I cobbled up an excuse that satisfied the Sunday editor of the Providence *Journal* to do a long piece on the battle for hegemony between the governor and the Speaker, using as my closer the fact that the *Journal* was then most interested in expanding its readership in southeastern Massachusetts communities bordering Rhode Island. I knew how the story would come out: Peabody would appear in shining armor, Thompson in manacles and fetters. It didn't happen that way; Thompson's mother could have written that story, if she loved him. One of the things we have to learn is to forgive the ignorances of the people that we were when we were young.

And another of the things we have to do is let the characters tell their own story, whether we are writing reportage or fiction. I let Thompson tell his own story in the *Journal*—I did have sense enough for that—and I locked away in my cerebrum (or perhaps, given Thompson's character, my cerebellum or id) the material he gave me for the other story I would write one day, when I got good enough, about a man patterned on him (I had, after all, read *All the King's Men,* and I knew within an instant of meeting him that as Robert Penn Warren had met his Huey Long, so I had just acquired my John Forbes Thompson).

The story simmered on the back burner of my head for almost twenty years. I knew it was there, like money in the bank, and I knew I had better not touch it until I was competent to handle it. The first thing to remember when you get a great idea for a story or a novel is that you must not waste it. There is some mysterious process of acquisition and assimilation that governs propitiousness in the composition of fiction. I do not claim to understand its terms or operation, but I know there is one. I did not use what I learned from John Forbes Thompson in 1962 until I started writing about Bernie Morgan in 1982, in what became *A Choice of Enemies.* It was not time until then. I do not know why it happened to be 1982, instead of 1981 or 1978, or 1989, when the time came to use what Thompson had taught me, but I do know, beyond a peradventure of a doubt, that it was 1982, and that it took me a very long time to put that novel through four drafts (on a Smith Corona electric typewriter—this was before I surrendered tardily and reluctantly, which was stupid of me, to the advance of technology, and acquired at least marginal proficiency with a word processor), and that when I had finished at last I knew that I had finally done something that I had had to do ever since the day I met that mean-tempered son of a bitch, and there was peace.

There ought to be a lesson in there somewhere about recognizing Henry James's *donnée* when you get it, and there probably is, but I don't know where it is. Some things—people, incidents, chance remarks—adhere to the memory the way winged insects do to flypaper, and then a day comes when perhaps you are trying to write about something that has nothing whatsoever to do with that experience from years ago, and it comes to a boil and you write about it. So what I am going to do now is take one of my own stories, not because I think it necessarily belongs in such company as a story by O'Hara (although of course I do) and walk you through its genesis, an escort service that I cannot perform with a story written by anyone else. The instruction that I hope you will get out of this, if you want to be a published writer, seems general and abstract, but in operation it is specific, material, and demanding. It is that you must pay attention at all times, especially when you do not want to pay attention and are somewhat impatient about what is going on, because irritation is nature's way of nudging us, and the incidents that irritate us are important.

My godmother was my second cousin, the daughter of my father's mother's sister. Her name was Emily E. Kendregan and she taught school all her working life and saved her money. She never married, depending first upon my grandfather and then upon my father to advise her on all matters about which she had doubts. Both of those men died before she did, which left her dependent upon me for such advice. I was not good at it, and both of us knew it, but I was mindful of my obligations and did the best I could. And when I got my law degree, and became a state prosecutor, she appeared to be convinced that I was trustworthy.

Emily was frugal. Like most frugal people she was a setup for a pitchman who could convince her that by spending a sum of money today, she would avert the expenditure of a much greater sum tomorrow. Sometime in 1967 or '68, some men in a red pickup truck unbidden visited Emily's house. They informed her they had inspected her asphalt driveway and judged it had been about ten or twelve years since it had been resurfaced. These were not stupid men; they had the age of the surface almost exactly right. They told her that it required resealing before the New England winter came around, or else it would erode badly under the multiple on-slaughts of snow, ice, plows, and salt. That was also true. They told her it would cost around twelve hundred dollars to have the work done by a pavement contractor specializing in town, county, and state highway resurfacing, but that since they did only driveways, on a free-lance basis, they could do the job for her for somewhere around four or five hundred dollars. They specified that they could afford to do such work so cheaply only by dealing strictly in cash, which Emily of course understood at once, because she didn't like credit ei-ther (if she suspected this also meant that they did not intend to pay taxes on their earnings, well, that would only have in-creased her trust; she always paid her taxes, but she didn't like it, one bit). They assuaged any misgivings she might have felt by assuring her that they did not expect any payment whatsoever until after they had finished their work, and she had inspected it and pronounced it satisfactory. She went for it on the spot.

The next day the men returned in the red pickup truck with several large drums of a black viscous substance that they carefully spread with push brooms over the asphalt. They were very neat and did not soil the grass bordering the drive-way, and when they were finished they blocked off the access from the street and asked her to look it over. She did so, and it was all black and shiny in the sun, and they asked her if she was satisfied, and she said that she was, and paid them four or five hundred dollars in cash. They cautioned her not to drive or walk on the newly treated asphalt for forty-eight hours, and then they left.

On the morning of the third day, when Emily walked on the driveway to her car in the garage, she ruined first her shoes and then the carpeting mats in her car. The black viscous liquid had not dried. Furthermore—as I learned when she got in touch with me to state her suspicion that she had been swindled, and I repeated her story to the state cops that I worked with—it wasn't going to. Ever. "Motor oil," they said. "Crankcase drippings. Guys're gypsies. They come around every three, four years or so, pull that scam on old people. What you've got to do is get it cleaned up. Phosphates. Cost a lot of money." And they told me some other scams that the gypsies like to run.

It cost Emily about $350 to remove the crankcase drippings from her driveway. I would've sued someone in her behalf, had there been someone to sue, but the reason gypsies do so well in their small frauds and thefts is that you can never find them afterward, to sue them. And if you could, well, gypsies never have any money that you could collect in damages. They have been doing this sort of thing for hundreds of years and they know the rackets better than the people that they work the rackets on.

Late in the summer of 1987, on a sunny Sunday morning, I took a much-deserved dip in the blasted swimming pool that came with my house and has cost me plenty, you bet, and then in my robe returned to the house, put on the coffee—no anisette; I'm not partial to that stuff—and went for the papers. After the motor ratcheted the garage door up and I had collected the papers, two white station wagons pulled into my drive, both of them loaded with adults and kids, and I thought at once of the gypsies that bilked Emily. Only now I knew I had a story, and I did not spend much more time outside that lovely day. I wrote "A Small Matter of Consumer Protection," published by *Playboy* in May 1988.

"Ah, Brother Shoate," Dennis Carnes said in the crowded concourse outside the District Courtrooms, "and what brings you out at this ungodly hour to this din of inequity? Dressed up like a regular bandleader—as usual, I might add." Teenagers in jeans and tank tops jostled each other in the line outside the probation office while they waited to state their names and home addresses for the later purpose of the judge setting bail. Aloof from them and sneering stood five men in their middle twenties, their hair long and greasy, their leather vests studded and carrying insignia consisting of a grinning red devil carrying a naked blonde woman, and the legend: *Satan's Apostles*. As far away as possible from both groups, and self-consciously apart from each other, were two teenaged girls, and four men in their late thirties, wearing suits and shirts and ties.

"The matter of making a living, Dinnis," Robert Shoate said, "and a tedious business it is."

Carnes arched his bushy eyebrows. "'A living,' is it?" he said. "And you as I get it representing a number of prominent members, the community, engaged in a variety of enterprises making fortunes, except when they get shut down by the authorities? 'United States of America versus Gelato Marinara—interstate racketeering': that's your bailiwick. No living for you to be made in these poor surroundings, Robbo, not by your lofty standards. Disturbing the peace? Drunks and disorderlies? Drivin' unders, and guys who whack their wives? Public urinators? You spend two hours in these shabby precincts, you'll lose what'd be a week's pay for guys like me, compared to what you're makin' on your fat arse in your office. Get out of here and leave the garbage to poor scavengers like me—we're used to going through the barrels—come here from the farce of habit, and we don't mind the stink. But you, you'll ruin that fine suit. Have to go home and take a hot bath before you can go back to work."

Shoate sighed. "Put your mind at ease, Dinnis," he said. He jerked his head to the left. "My client's down by the door," he said.

Carnes peered over Shoate's shoulder. He saw a man about seventy in a silvery-grey suit that matched his wavy hair. "Don't recognize him," he said. "Don't belong in here, though—that I recognize. What's the charge?"

"A small consumer protection matter," Shoate said.

"That's a civil thing," Carnes said. "Civil don't start 'till eleven. This's the criminal session. See what happens, you guys in the swell suits, start working our side of the street? Right off the bat, you start making mistakes, showing your ignorance."

"My client's particular consumer protection matter," Shoate said, "happens to be criminal. My consumer protected himself. A and B, DW's the charge. Five adults and their wee small children claim he fired a shotgun at them."

"My goodness," Carnes said. "What's the fuckin' world coming to, nice-lookin' gentleman like that starts firing on other civilians?"

"That's almost what he says," Shoate said. "His version is: 'Fuck's going on, man has to keep a shotgun handy just to live in his own house?'"

"Did he do it?" Carnes said.

"Yup," Shoate said. "Just between you and me, of course. And not just once, either. He's got one of those Remington Bushmaster Twelves, with the just-legal barrel, and he loaded her up and emptied the magazine—six full ounces of steel shot."

"So it wasn't a mistake, then," Carnes said. "He didn't think they were pheasants or something."

"Nope," Shoate said. "He thought they were gypsies."

"Jesus," Carnes said, "what is it, legal shoot gypsies now?

130

Who is this fellow, anyway? Adolf goddamned Hitler or something?"

"Well, now," Shoate said, "let's be careful here. He didn't actually *shoot* them. But he came near enough so they thought he had that in mind. Little do they know. When this guy misses, it's because he *wants* to miss."

"Then why'd he shoot at them, he wanted to miss?" Carnes said.

"To get them off of his land," Shoate said. "And also: out of his pool."

"They doing on his land?" Carnes said. "Bangin' their tambourines at him?"

Shoate laughed. "Look," he said, "he's retired. He's mostly retired. He's got a nice big house at the foot of a lane, out at the end of the Point. Got the ocean from his windows, and the lighthouse—all of that. You know how it is with these older guys: Likes to get up early, take a swim in his pool, get his robe on and go out, get the papers from the yard. And you know how the paperboys are—papers're always 'way the hell down the driveway.

"So he does that, Saturday morning. Finishes the swim, gets the terry robe on, opens the garage door and goes out and gets the papers. Coffee's making, he's got the little glass of anisette on the dining room table—hey, why the hell not, all right? Enjoy his life? What's wrong with that—he's retired."

"Especially since most your clients, his old pals, they get retired, they're down in Atlanta," Carnes said. "He's a lucky man."

Shoate chuckled. "Well," he said, "he's got a good lawyer, and he usually does what his lawyer tells him. Which the guys that went south didn't always do. But that's another matter.

"The door opens and he goes out in the driveway and picks up the papers. Got to keep track, his investments, stocks and bonds and all that stuff. And he's going back in the garage, and up come these two cars. Couple white Dodge wagons with the wood on the sides? And down around the corner, he sees this red pick-up truck pull up.

"'Jesus, Bobby,' he says, 'it's like the clown cars in the circus. I'm standing there in my robe and my slippers, and these two cars pull in my driveway, and all these people start getting out. Big people, little people—it's like a fuckin' rally, something. And the daddies start rubbing their hands on my driveway, you know? Their knuckles. And the mummies—I assume they're the mummies—start unloading the trikes from the cars, and it's like a fuckin' magic act. All of a sudden I got about eleven people swarming all over my driveway. And I think: "What the *fuck?*" And then I know: Gypsies.'"

"'Gypsies,'" Carnes said. "How's he know they're gypsies?"

"Because they come back, like locusts," Shoate said. "Every four, five years, they come around again, and they cheat people. They especially like old people. They don't tell them they're gypsies. They tell them their roof's coming off, and they'll fix it for twelve hundred bucks. 'Gonna have a lotta bad leaks here, Lady, don't get them shingles nailed down.' They tell them their trees're all dying. 'Get a good windstorm here, Mister, gonna knock all your power lines down.' And they come in for one day, whole army of people, and they climb all over your roof, hammering like hell. Or they get a whole buncha people and cut off a whole bunch of limbs. And that night they leave, with half of your money—they wanted it all, but you're not that dumb: 'The rest when you finish the job.' And that's the last you see of them. If it was the roof scam, your yard's full of nails, half the shingles're off of your roof. If it was the tree scam, your yard's full of branches and your trees look like they're half-dressed. And you never see them again. And nobody else finds them, either.

"Well," Shoate said, "this year it's asphalt driveways. 'You better seal that driveway, Mister. Gonna lose the whole thing, the next rain. Four hundred, good as new. Finish in a day. We'll be here tomorrow. Gotta be cash—we're non-union help.' Meaning: 'We don't pay no taxes.' Wink, wink. 'Twice as much if we were.' So the addled old bastard goes to the bank, gets the money in hundreds, and the next day the gypsies show up with a buncha highway cones they stole, and they block off the driveway and get out their brooms, and spread the whole thing with crankcase drippings.''

"Used motor oil?" Carnes said. "I never heard of that sealing driveways.''

"It doesn't," Shoate said. "But because you do what they tell you, and stay off it forty-eight hours, you don't find that out for two days. Then you find out what the oil does is get on your shoes, and you track it in the house, the wall-to-wall, and the carpeting, your car, and it takes about three hundred pounds of phosphates, wash the damned stuff off, and that costs you another nine hundred bucks, and the meantime the gypsies're off to another town, playing their sad violins, dancing around in the firelight.

"The whole theory is: they intimidate you. They arrive like an army and they get these old people, well-off, naturally, but still old. And all of a sudden these elderly people are surrounded by a bunch of jabbering bastards telling them their house is going down the hill if something isn't done real soon. The people that get cheated, about twenty minutes after they get taken, it dawns on them, what's gone on. But by then it's too late—the gypsies're gone. Nothing a soul can do.

"This is a good theory—until the guy you pick to intimidate is my guy. He does not intimidate. He used to, so he knows how it's done, and he knows a scam when he sees one. Furthermore, he knows knowledge is power, and that's why he reads the newspapers. Especially the local police blotter reports.

"He retreats the garage, and he hits the door button, and two their eight kids or so ride their trikes in. And he says to them, in his best kindly fashion—it happens to be Gospel truth: 'Inna house I got the biggest goddamned kid-eating dog you ever saw in your life. Either get out the garage, 'fore the door's alla way down, or stay the garage—wait for him. And he will fuckin' *eat*

133

you.' Which he would. Dog's a fuckin' Rottweiler, 'bout the same size as Goliath. So the kids screw, and the door goes down, and he figures he's rid of the bastards.

"He's not. 'They're *stupid*,' he says me. 'No brains at all. The next thing I know, I look outta my window, the bastards're all in my pool. The kids anyway at least are. I got three strands of barbed wire, top of my fence, and those fuckers got in over it. Now I think to myself: "Hey, what's going on?" And then: "What do I do about it?"'

"'Now,' he says, 'I know from the cops. I been through this routine before. You call up the cops: 'There're kids in my pool.' The cops say: 'Serve 'em a snack.' They'll do nothing for you, guy like I am, do nothing for nobody else. Last thing they want's a good wrestling match, some kids climbed the fence to your pool. They're whooping and hollering, raising all hell, my wife's trying to sleep, and who invited these shits?

"'So I go inna closet and get out the gun, and load up the son of a bitch. Then I open the back door, go out on the deck, and start taking a few practice shots. Took a couple branches off the dogwood and I trimmed the willow some, but it's all in a good cause. About the third shot I see people running, fast. So I cut back the spruce next the driveway, and I hear the cars starting up. And I went back in the house, and that's all I did. Honest to Christ, that is all.'"

"Has he got a permit?" Carnes said.

"Why's he need a permit?" Shoate said. "He had the gun before the law changed. Doesn't carry it. Keep it in his own home, protection life and property? Doesn't need a license. He's all right on the gun law—it's the people law's his trouble."

"Well, he's gonna get bound over," Carnes said. "Cop gets onna stand, reads his report of that, Judge Feeley isn't gonna have no choice: 'Off to the grand jury, Guido—take your chances there.'"

"Ah," Shoate said, "but that's where I come in. The cop's not reading his report. Saturday afternoon I went down the station and I said: 'Now look, all right? I just want to tell you, so you don't think I pulled a fast one when my guy gets arraigned. I'm gonna call for eyewitness testimony, which you guys don't happen to be. And I know you're gonna say you've got a sworn complaint, and hearsay's good enough PC to bind my client over. Good enough probable cause, far's that goes, to get a damned indictment. But then there's gonna be a trial, because my guy will not fold. And then the DA's gonna have to crank up some real live witnesses. You think they're gonna show up for that? These bastards'll be in Oklahoma by then, swindling innocent cowboys.'

"And the lieutenant looks at me," Shoate said, "and he says: 'We can't dismiss the thing, you know. That gets in the papers, everyone in town'll say we're in the bag, your guy. Selectmen'll be bullshit, looks like we took a walk.'

" 'It won't,' I say. 'All I want you to do between now and Monday's try to find the victims. That's all—just try to locate them. And if you can't, and I ask you, just tell the truth—that's all.' "

"You figured they'd be gone?" Carnes said.

"Oh, I *knew* they'd be gone," Shoate said. " 'Bobby,' my guy says, yesterday lunchtime, calls me up out at the pool: 'I had some people, find out these bastards're staying. Hot-pillow joint, over Quincy. About eight of them to a room. And you know what? The strangest thing happened. They get up this morning, go out inna lot, their cars and their truck disappeared. So they're raisin' a big stink and head for the office—they're gonna call the police. They get in the office, the manager hands them a note. They can't even *read* it. Here're these bastards, out cheating people, they can't even read a fuckin' note. Desk guy reads it to them. And they look at each other, and I guess the first thing, crosses their mind, is find out whether it's true."

" 'So they all go tearin' out the door again,' he says, and he's laughing like hell, of course, now, 'and they go down the river like the note says, and sure enough, there's the truck, under about five feet salt water. And on the other side the river, over in the marsh, there're the white cars. Up to their bumpers in mud. And I guess then they believe what the note says: "Noon today, the tide comes in. You don't get them cars out by then, you never get them out. And when you get those cars out, then you get in them and get out. You better not come back."'

"So," Shoate said, "they got a wrecker on the double, winched the cars back on the road, took them down the car wash—my guy's guy watching all this—hose them down and screw. 'The last he seen of them, Bobby, they're headed west, real fast.'"

Carnes frowned. "I can't maybe put my finger right on it," he said, "but there's just the slightest smell here, maybe justice got obstructed."

"By who?" Shoate said. "My guy wasn't there. I wasn't there. Just happened to be a guy, knows my guy, and all he did was look on. Nothing wrong with that. Perfectly legal thing. Some tourists come in, their plans suddenly change—some young punks think it's funny, sink their truck in a river. So they decide we're a lawless community. They leave town sooner'n planned. You've seen those American Express ads—happens all the time. Besides, you know those happy gypsies—footlose bastards they are—always on the move, looking for a peaceful town."

Carnes stared at him. He nodded. "And all these years," he said, "I think the reason you're getting all the heavies is because you're so goddamned good. And it isn't. The reason you get all the heavies is because you let the heavies do all the lifting, and you're just the guy out in front, takin' all the bows."

Shoate laughed. He clapped Carnes on the shoulder. "Hey, Dinnis," he said, "long's the music comes out sounding good, I'll be willing to lead the damned band."

Have in mind now what O'Hara said about the need for accuracy in dialogue. Dennis Carnes addressed Robert Shoate as "Brother Shoate." The elaborate formalities of the courtroom, devised and enforced to avoid unseemly fistfights, in the chauvinist days of yore engendered the custom of referring to one's adversary as "my learned brother." This was a serviceable expression because it always looks respectfully the same on the printed transcript page. But the person who utters it can convey quite a different meaning by tone and enunciation. Spoken in an offhand manner, it politely acknowledges the judge's right to demand decorum, and vouchsafes professional respect for one's opponent. Voiced dripping with sarcasm—as in: "If my learned brother ever knew the rules of evidence, he has obviously forgotten them" —it functions both to alert the judge to one's animosity toward and contempt for his opponent, and may serve as well to light the other fellow's fuse, so that he loses enough of his command of his wits to distract him from full command of his case.

Carnes calls Shoate "Brother" in the latter mode, which indicates to the initiated that he does not admire Shoate, and in fact harbors some hostility toward him. Is this, for the common reader, what Jacques Barzun condemned as "pseudo-jargon" in "The Language of Learning and of Pedantry" (collected among the essays in his book *The House of Intellect,* 1959)? No, this is real jargon, and Barzun said this well enough so that there is no need to improve on it. "Jargon is the special vocabulary of a trade or art. The terms are fixed and they exist because none other will do." The jargon of trial lawyers is important to a story that is meant for the common reader—who may very well be a trial lawyer, given the profusion of the species nowadays—because it authenticates the speakers of the dialogue as members of that profession. One need not be a mechanic, or have any idea of how mechanics do whatever they do, in order to understand that a person comfortably employing the word *camshaft* in workaday conversation knows at least the rudiments of work as a mechanic, and who accordingly warrants trust when he or she talks about internal combustion engines.

Trust is what the fiction writer needs from the reader, because the writer is trying to make the reader believe what both of them know in the abstract to be a pack of lies. The fiction must therefore be plausible. The code words, and the usage of the initiates, validate the fiction, even for the person who has never used them and is not really sure what they mean—data, data, data.

Carnes describes the setting as a "din of inequity." This is a double pun. I stole it. A friend of mine, Frank Burns, operates the A Street Scrap Metal Yard on Fourth and A Street in South Boston. He reads everything and listens attentively. He called me one day to report that a cop had used that phrase to describe the morning uproar in the South Boston District Court, nicely ringing a change on the cliché "den of iniquity." I told Frank at once that I would steal it at the first opportunity, as of course I did. I didn't reckon at the time that it would suggest to me Carnes's next pun—"the farce of habit," from "the force of habit"—but it did, and I don't reject lagniappes.

Shoate pronounces "Dennis" as "Dinnis." This is a deliberate act committed by Irish-Americans who wish to establish either that they have not forgotten their humble origins— "gone high-hat on us" is the term for that—or wish to warn off tormentors of similar ancestry by reminding them that however much the speaker may be deservedly envied his relative prosperity, he retains inside the fine suit a hearty understanding of the Game and the Rules, and is not to be trifled with. A variant is "me mither," for "my mother." It means exactly the same thing as the correct pronunciation, but carries with it as well the imputation of whatever irony the speaker wishes to deliver.

Shoate has reason to defend himself against Carnes. Carnes obviously envies Shoate's prosperity as a Mafia lawyer and expresses it by sneering at him, disparaging his generic client as "Gelato Marinara." Gelato is an ice dessert, a form of sherbet; marinara is tomato-based pasta sauce.

Carnes has not come right out and said that he thinks Shoate's munificent clients remain nonetheless a bunch of lowlifes, nor has he scorned Shoate explicitly for his willingness to represent such evildoers, let alone consort with Italians (nasty little ethnic slur, in that fabricated name)—of course he hasn't, because he doesn't need to. And Carnes calls Shoate "Robbo," a finely tuned insult both eponymous —he is robbing his disreputable clients—and class-hostile: lawyers operating on Shoate's level use full Christian names only sparingly, with only the closest of colleagues, and almost never use diminutives. Carnes is cutting Shoate down to size, or attempting to, at least.

Carnes fails. Shoate, by deprecating the necessity for his appearance in a lowly district court, crowded with motorcycle gang members and, as Carnes calls them, "public urinators," establishes that his "small consumer protection matter" requires his attendance for precisely the reason that prompts Carnes to envy him: Shoate represents a retired Mafia don who has had some trouble with gypsies. Just as my godmother did, but Godfathers handle such intrusions more decisively than spinster cousins do.

That brings us to the issue of just what magic it is that Shoate proposes to do for his beneficent client, who clearly did what the police have charged him with doing. This is important to Carnes, who has obviously gloated when others among Shoate's clientele of hoods have been carted off to the federal correctional facility at Atlanta, Georgia—more jargon here: Atlanta was a maximum security facility, and you only went there if you were a very bad boy indeed, sentenced to spend a long time repenting the fact that you had been caught at it. Shoate deftly deflects Carnes's thrust: the "guys that went south didn't always do" what their lawyer advised them to do. Shoate is playing with Carnes the way a well-mannered house dog "kills" a cooked pork chop by flinging it around and pretending to break its neck before eating it. He condescends to instruct Carnes on the habits of the gypsies, and the operations they conduct in the commission of their frauds. The clear implication (well, it's clear to me, at least) is that Shoate patronizingly considers that the proudly street-savvy Carnes (remember Carnes's crack that Shoate should leave the rubbish cases to the seedy hacks who are used to going through the barrels) really doesn't know anywhere near as much as he believes he does. And therefore should have thought twice before he suggested that Shoate is some sort of a manicured fop who does not belong in the trench-warfare setting of the district court.

As Shoate warms to his own defense, he deliberately vulgarizes his syntax to match Carnes's. Near the beginning, Shoate speaks in full sentences: "Put your mind at ease, Dinnis," and "My client's down by the door." He continues to do so until Carnes first uses the magic word: "What's the *fuckin'* world coming to, nice-lookin' gentleman like that starts firing on other civilians?"

In this context, as in the vast majority of other situations, conversational or written, in which the word is used today, it is a mere intensifier with absolutely no sexual denotation or connotation whatsoever. Its employment in such exchanges as this one serves chiefly to express the speaker's attitude toward shocking the listener: the speaker either does not expect the listener will be shocked (thus implying that the listener is as coarse and hardened as the speaker), does not care whether the listener will be shocked (thus conveying the speaker's disdain for the listener) or that the listener, unshocked, will be obliged to demonstrate he is not shocked (either by comfortably descending to the same level or by haughtily and ostentatiously rising to a higher one). Confrontation is under way here, as it almost always is when two trial lawyers, not especially admiring each other, compulsively compete to see who is the tougher and more resourceful adversary.

Shoate wins this round. He is not shocked. But he avoids Carnes's trap for the unshocked by using *fuck* in indirect quotation of his client. Shoate, in other words, feels no dismay at uttering the word, but implies he does so only when attributing its usage to someone not as cultivated as he. In short, Shoate in two sentences first finesses Carnes's trick, and then neatly puts him in the same category with the Mafioso for whom Carnes has manifested contempt.

Carnes now retreats into a display of sincere curiosity, part of which is genuine and part of which is an acknowledgment that Shoate has successfully defended himself against Carnes's hostile harassment. Shoate is gracious in victory. Not only does he provide an entertaining account of events leading to the prosecution; he also delivers them in the same disorderly grammar and syntax in which Carnes initiated the contest. Shoate's implication is that he has won, and will now show himself to be a good fellow with no hard feelings about Carnes's attack. Shoate omits prepositions—"He retreats [into] the garage. . . ." He quotes several times his client's use of the word *fuck,* and even employs it once himself—but only once. The implication is this: "I'm not afraid of it. I just don't need it."

The purpose of all this new camaraderie on Shoate's part is to convey two lessons to Carnes. Both of them are about intimidation, to establish that a smart, tough fellow expects respect, and knows how to enforce it when it's foolishly withheld.

The first lesson is that the gypsies believed they could intimidate Shoate's client, but instead were first intimidated by him—scared out of their wits, in fact—because Shoate's client is an experienced intimidator in his own right, and better at the game, and then, when the gypsies went to the police to start a second attack, they were driven right out of town. They were guilty of disrespect.

The second is that Carnes, embarking at the very outset of

the story on an effort to intimidate Shoate and make him feel himself an unwelcome intruder—"Dressed up like a regular bandleader—as usual, I might add"—in the district court, has shown poor judgment similar to that displayed by the gypsies in selecting the Mafioso as a helpless victim. Shoate is willing to be decent about Carnes's futile effort to overbear him, but he desires Carnes to understand that it had better not happen again, because there is a reason why Shoate has the money to buy the fancy suits: his client is smarter and tougher than Carnes's miscreants are, and Shoate is smarter and tougher than Carnes. And the proof of that, which Shoate presses upon Carnes, is that Shoate forewarned the police that their witnesses had decamped, thus enabling the police to avoid the embarrassment of later bringing an indictment they would surely lose. Shoate shows respect to his adversaries, as Carnes does not, and that is why the music sounds good.

Until I started teaching writing at the university level, the only colloquies I had with readers and prospective writers were those that occurred in the question-and-answer sessions that I like to conduct at the close of guest lectures and library readings. Because those encounters were necessarily brief, and by their terms discouraged the shy from putting their questions while at the same time limiting the ability of the bold to pursue lines of inquiry that they deemed promising, I quite inadvertently misled some people who deserved better. It was not until I began to lead extended small seminars each week (at the State University of New York at Buffalo in 1988) that the actual nature of the questions I had fielded superficially at libraries and in lecture halls dawned on me; those questions were a little more complicated than I had understood. When people inquire of writers—well, of this writer, at least—where they "get the ideas for the stories," they are assuming that the story they have just read or heard existed entirely, as an idea, before I started writing it.

But the fact is that it didn't; the only "idea" that I had when I sat down to write "A Small Matter of Consumer Protection" that Sunday morning was that if the gypsies who cheated Emily, and got away with it, had instead chosen as their victim a surly, savvy, retired gangster who had a shotgun handy and no compunction about using it, the enterprise would have turned out quite differently.

By the time I had finished coffee and the Sunday papers, showered off the chlorine, and put on my work clothes, I had dealt with the likely consequences of discharging a shotgun at trespassers. Prosecution would be almost certain. Therefore the don, having dismissed the gypsies, would probably find himself in need of counsel. The question that remained was how on earth a lawyer would successfully defend his client on such an open-and-shut case.

I didn't know the answer to that question until Shoate related the second call from his client, reporting that the gypsies had decided to leave town. The rest came easy.

It was not until I had let the story cool for a day or two (I find that good practice, because the distraction of quotidian matters of any trade lets the practitioner review his work with comparative freshness; I let several weeks elapse after completing each draft of a novel, because the process of writing them is so protracted over weeks or months that I need more time for recovery of perspective) that I saw for the first time the symmetry between what Shoate had done to Carnes and what the don had done to the gypsies. So I rewrote the story with that in mind, and that was the draft that was published.

The point of all this is that the answer to "Where do you get the idea for a story?" depends completely on what the questioner means by "idea" and by "story." I get first the idea that causes me to sit down and write. And when I see what I have written, I get the idea for the story I send out.

7

It is not often that someone comes along who is a true friend and a good writer. Charlotte was both.

—E. B. White, *Charlotte's Web*

The source of the data is not anywhere near as important as the understanding of what they actually mean. E. B. White secured his data for his classic by studying life on the farm in Maine where he spent his summers, thinking about what happened to pigs that became family pets while being raised for market, and then about what happened to the industrious spiders after they had spun the intricate webs that caught their food and left the eggs that would mature in the spring to hatch new spiders. He observed that the rats that scavenged in the barn subsisted on food that they stole from its intended recipients, and he thought about how a little girl would feel in the course of the summer leading up to her discovery that the power of love might be overmatched against the power of doom, and that was what he wrote about.

Brazenly (which may account for his success) he flouted the convention forbidding serious writers to attribute exclusively human characteristics—the ability to think, for example—to inanimate objects, nature, and the other, lower animals, obtaining his license to ignore the ban against anthropomorphism by depending confidently upon the power of his imagination to beguile his reader into overlooking the offense. And his confidence was rewarded. If you, as I, were born too soon before Harper & Row published the story in 1952 for your parents to have read it aloud to you, or if you reached the age of three or four after 1952 but they omitted to do the right thing, get a copy for yourself soon, and repair their oversight. Under the impression that it was merely a story for toddlers, I did not read it myself until mine were old enough to love it, in the early seventies; they went to bed peacefully enough after hearing the first chapter, but I ignored some legal work I had brought home to finish *Charlotte* that night.

The principal reason for the charm of the story, I think, is White's respect for the dignity of his characters, regardless of their actual status as human, porcine, arachnid, or rodent. Beatrix Potter, committing the same indiscretion in her tales of Peter Rabbit, his family, and acquaintances, succeeded for the same reason. I suppose the general lesson here for writers is substantially the same as the best counsel for adulterers: People watching what you do will not have much trouble figuring out that you are sinning, so you may as well go about it with as much boldness and *duende* as you can muster, and see if you can bring it off.

The specific lessons include this: It is not a good idea to take sides among your characters, no matter how stylishly you may plan to do it, unless you are absolutely sure that you are skillful enough to conceal your bias completely from your reader. This rule is new, reflecting the responsibilities that devolved upon writers of fiction in the aftermath of World

War I, as the price of our gradually expanding freedoms. Now, if you want to set yourself up in judgment of your characters—who are, after all, helpless in your control—you should abandon serious fiction and take up composition of political, religious, or other hortatory stuff.

The explanation is quite straightforward. If you try to rig your stories to enable the characters that you like to prevail over those that you don't, your readers will almost invariably spot it. Then they will dismiss not only the message of the parable you have set out to tell them, but the parable itself. They will in effect allege that you defrauded them, purporting to offer them a story and then trying to slip in a lecture in its place. O'Hara had some worthwhile observations on this point when he gave a speech at Foyle's bookstore in London on May 3, 1967 (collected in *John O'Hara on Writers and Writing*). "I was distressed some years ago to discover that the works of Damon Runyon were enjoying a vogue in England, and that there was a cult of Runyonadoes who affected Runyonesque speech in the entirely erroneous belief that there were people who talked that way. The thing that I disliked most about Runyon's writing was its fundamental dishonesty. I knew Runyon and I knew the people he had in mind when he was writing. They were no damned good. They were thieves and chiselers, and if any of them had had a heart of gold it would have been cut out of them by their companions. The sad thing is that Runyon could have been a social historian; no one knew the gangsters and the gamblers and the pimps and prostitutes better than he, and he could write. But he never told the truth about them. He gave them a sort of raffish innocence. . . ," and if you want to see what O'Hara had in mind when he said that, catch a rerun or a video cassette of *Guys and Dolls*, the delightful music by Frank Loesser incongruously issuing from the lungs of Runyon's phony hoods. Enjoy the music; don't even try to believe the story.

This does not mean that you must never find the antics of your characters amusing, or even hilarious. And that of course brings us by the back way into thinking about what is involved in writing stories that turn out to be funny—as opposed to Runyon's labored efforts, which were meant to be funny, and therefore weren't—and what all that might mean.

What it means is that the laughs must develop from the reader's observation of the fun that they are having, at their own expense or that of other characters, not from the fun that you are having at their expense. If anything, the writer's obligation to stay out of the amusing event is greater than his duty to remain aloof from the one that is solemn. This is because most humor is cruel. It is okay for characters to be cruel to each other, but when the writer is cruel to them, that is bullying.

I can think of no American writer better suited to illustration of that premise than Ring Lardner (who greatly preferred that form of address to his baptismal names of Ringgold Wilmer, and understandably so). Lardner, as was common for writers of his generation (1885–1933), endured no formal schooling beyond the secondary level, which, I surmise, both burdened him with less prechewed stylistic and technical baggage than late-twentieth-century American writers have often had to jettison before they could get to work, and deprived him of the training that contributes heavily to the writer's ability to conceive book-length stories. He gravitated toward the sports beat as a journalist, drawn by the anomaly implied by the simultaneity of public veneration of ballplayers as objects of esteem and their actual existences as uncouth, unlettered louts, as amorally naive on the subjects of personal morals and ethics as they were blissfully unaware of the lucrative degree to which their greedy employers were making financial saps of them, and fortunes for themselves (for a splendid biography of Lardner, see *Ring*, by Jonathan Yardley, 1977; for a riveting factual account of how organized baseball before, during, and after the 1919 Black Sox scandal chewed up and spat out the men it used for fodder, see Eliot Asinof's *Eight Men Out,* Henry Holt and Co., reissued in paperback in 1988, the basis for the 1988 John Sayles movie of the same name).

That professional development, I think, accounts for the fact that Lardner never produced a publishable novel. He had been trained from an early age to think in terms of the daily gouts of short prose—eight hundred to one thousand words —that newspapers deliver to their readers. Ideally, if far from always, those dispatches are rhetorically complete, including in their brief spans a beginning, middle and end—the end being by far the least important of the three, since editors cramped for space and pressed for time have since the memory of man runneth not to the contrary exercised the Procrustean option by cutting ruthlessly from the bottom of copy that won't otherwise fit. When Lardner became sufficiently chafed by such newspapering constraints to venture into the realm of fiction, he seemed literally unable to extend a narrative much beyond three thousand words. One doubts that he suffered overmuch from this limitation, if that was what it was; the returns from his work in the 1920s would amount to more than five hundred thousand of today's inflated dollars, and Congress at that point had not yet fully appreciated the near-confiscatory powers inhering in the Sixteenth Amendment, which upon ratification by three-quarters of the states in 1913 enabled passage of laws imposing federal taxes upon incomes. But it is still hard today to avoid wistful regret that he did not write novels.

Such mopishness aside, Lardner merits reading by today's aspiring writer because, better than virtually anyone else, he worked the dangerous verge where mordant humor pushed too far degenerates into the kind of appalling, mendacious caricature that O'Hara deplored in Runyon's work. His best, to subscribe for once to a consensus, is "Haircut," which will repay your efforts to track it down at the library or locate it in reprint at your bookstore. Pending that exertion, this précis may serve.

The story is a traveler's report of his visit to a small town. The principal elements are these: Jim Kendall has been killed. Whitey, the stupid barber (an occupation known then and known today for its tendency to attract the garrulous), feeling himself obligated to provide a new customer with diversion as well as a trim, propounds the view that Kendall, with the assistance of Hod Meyers, amounted to a cherished local resource of hilarity. In Whitey's stated view, Kendall's death seriously diminished the quality of life, the "pretty good times," in the little town. The reader's natural curiosity is aroused; he would like to know what remarkable feats Kendall performed to merit such post-mortem admiration. Lurking under that is the reader's natural if malicious skepticism: Whitey has twice warned him that the community cannot compete with New York or Chicago as an entertainment mecca, thus raising the reader's distinct suspicion that he is in for a yokel's report of gallus-snapping antics unfunny except to an audience of other yokels (all readers are snobs, and the shrewd author panders to that innate if rebuttable assurance of superior sophistication); he surmises that he may very well end up laughing at Whitey, rather than with him.

Uncultivated as Whitey is, he nevertheless perceives that he has volunteered to carry the burden of proving his premise that Jim Kendall was a regular card. His first offering is the evidence of the deference accorded Kendall by the other, lesser, wags who congregate in the barber shop on Saturday evenings: the big chair was deemed his, and all pretenders to that throne vacated it upon his arrival. Sensing that his listener, the reader, will require some justification for this manifestation of respect, Whitey, with pardonable vain care to demonstrate that he is something of a wit in his own right, offers his exchange with Kendall about excessive drinking (this takes place during Prohibition, keep in mind, when the puritanical ban on intoxicants made the subject a litmus test of masculine worthiness). It isn't funny at all, but even as it confirms the reader's initial suspicion that Whitey's taste in humor is less demanding than his own, it enables Whitey, with Hod's assistance, to convey the data that Kendall had a weakness for the booze, and a troubled marriage, too. Whereupon Whitey segues nicely into the interchange between Kendall and Meyers meanly ridiculing Milt Sheppard's physical shortcomings. A real thigh-slapper, that one, but it is more than that: it is the reader's first inkling of Kendall's taste for cruelty toward defenseless victims, and it begins his introduction as a bully.

It seems likely that if Lardner had employed a smoother, less oafish narrator, he could not have brought off Whitey's abrupt transition from the nastiness of Kendall's japes at Sheppard to the disclosure that Kendall's boorishness had resulted in his dismissal from his job as a traveling salesman of canned goods. It is a classic *non sequitur:* Lardner takes us via a display of shaving mugs directly into data confirming our preliminary estimate of Kendall, and then into description of Kendall's perverse boastfulness about his discharge. He brought it on himself by stirring up marital discord in each town on his route. The account conclusively establishes that Kendall, esteemed as an entertainer *manqué* in the barbershop, was in fact a disgusting lout whose idea of fun consisted of causing pain to others who had done him no harm, or even met him. Whitey, in his loquacious eagerness to win the visiting stranger (reader)'s approval of himself (by his gift of the story) and his simultaneous endorsement of Whitey's view that Kendall was a charmer in a discerning community, has now defeated both of his ambitions, revealing himself to be utterly obtuse and his hero to have been a malicious clod. Whitey has succeeded in fascinating the stranger (reader) but not in the manner that he had intended.

Making a bad thing worse, Whitey then establishes that Kendall's random cruelty to others was nowhere near as refined or as reprehensible as his vicious treatment of his wife and children. This, in Whitey's skewed narrative judgment, requires the introduction of Doctor Stair and the village idiot, Paul Dickson, the unlikely partners in the "accidental," rough poetic justice that makes an end to Kendall and his evil interference in other people's lives.

It is perfectly clear that if Lardner had not delivered that preposterous fable from the point of view he chose, he never would have gotten away with it. Eliminate Whitey and his earnest protestations that Kendall was a true comedian and you are left with a villainous monarch moonlighting as a dragon; a virtuous damsel in distress; a very perfect, gentle knight; and a defenseless fool. Only a bard of little brain could narrate so clichéd a ballad without being hooted off the stage. By pretending to introduce Whitey as a diverting raconteur, claiming the equal's right of sympathetic agreement in the premise that his village is—or at least was—thoroughly up-to-date, Lardner captured the audience for the revelation that the small-town life he knew about could be brutish, short, and nasty, appreciable only by a truly stupid man. Lardner was a merciless writer, and those are the best kind.

Equally merciless was James Thurber, whose nearly four decades (1927–1961) as a contributor to *The New Yorker* and freelance man-of-most-literary-trades yielded not only a splendid memoir of the magazine's founding eccentric, editor Harold Ross (*The Years with Ross*, 1959) but also twenty-two volumes of drawings, sketches, whimsies, essays, stories, collections, tales for children, and coauthorship with Elliot Nugent of a 1940 musical comedy—*The Male Animal*. This is not to say that Thurber, perhaps best known for his story "The Secret Life of Walter Mitty," imitated Lardner's tonal savagery; his work featured chiefly males bewildered by fierce women, and animals resignedly baffled by everything they encounter. His eyesight deserted him along with his youth, so the figures in his drawings, never exactly drafts-manlike, gradually became amorphous as he aged, visually reflecting the puzzled attitude that his characters plaintively evince in their reports of events that they have witnessed without fully understanding. "You Could Look It Up," Thurber's 1937 *Saturday Evening Post* story presaging, if not provoking, the 1951 publicity stunt staged by Bill Veeck, Jr. —the St. Louis Browns' owner engaged 3'7" midget Eddie Gaedell to work a base on balls in a regular-season (i.e., for the Browns, dismal) game—typified his gentle approach. He did not spare his subjects; it was just that the conduct that caught his attention was more feckless than brutish.

It all begun when we dropped down to C'lumbus, Ohio, from Pittsburgh to play a exhibition game on our way out to St. Louis. It was gettin' on into September, and though we'd been leadin' the league by six, seven games most of the season, we was now in first place by a margin you could 'a' got it into the eye of a thimble, bein' only a half a game ahead of St. Louis. Our slump had given the boys the leapin' jumps, and they was like a bunch a old ladies at a lawn fete with a thunderstorm comin' up, runnin' around snarlin' at each other, eatin' bad and sleepin' worse, and battin' for a team average of maybe .186. Half the time nobody'd speak to nobody else, without it was to bawl 'em out.

Squawks Magrew was managin' the boys at the time, and he was darn near crazy. They called him "Squawks" 'cause when things was goin' bad he lost his voice, or perty near lost it, and squealed at you like a little girl you stepped on her doll or somethin'. He yelled at everybody and wouldn't listen to nobody, without maybe it was me. I'd been trainin' the boys for ten year, and he'd take more lip from me than from anybody else. He knowed I was smarter'n him, anyways, like you're goin' to hear.

This was thirty, thirty-one year ago; you could look it up, 'cause it was the same year C'lumbus decided to call itself the Arch City, on account of a lot of iron arches with electric-light bulbs into 'em which stretched acrost High Street. Thomas Albert Edison sent 'em a telegram, and they was speeches and maybe even President Taft opened the celebration by pushin' a button. It was a great week for the Buckeye capital, which was why they got us out there for this exhibition game.

Well, we just lose a double-header to Pittsburgh, 11 to 5 and 7 to 3, so we snarled all the way to C'lumbus, where we put up at the Chittaden Hotel, still snarlin'. Everybody was tetchy, and when Billy Klinger took a sock at Whitey Cott at breakfast, Whitey throwed marmalade all over his face.

"Blind each other, whatta I care?" says Magrew. "You can't see nothin' anyways."

C'lumbus win the exhibition game, 3 to 2, whilst Magrew set in the dugout, mutterin' and cursin' like a fourteen-year-old Scotty. He bad-mouthed everybody on the ball club and he bad-mouthed everybody offa the ball club, includin' the Wright brothers, who, he claimed, had yet to build a airship big enough for any of our boys to hit it with a ball bat.

"I wisht I was dead," he says to me. "I wisht I was in heaven with the angels."

I told him to pull hisself together, 'cause he was drivin' the boys crazy, the way he was goin' on, sulkin' and bad-mouthin' and whinin'. I was older'n he was and smarter'n he was, and he knowed it. I was ten times smarter'n he was about this Pearl du Monville, first time I ever laid eyes on the little guy, which was one of the saddest days of my life.

Now, most people name of Pearl is girls, but this Pearl du Monville was a man, if you could call a fella a man who was only thirty-four, thirty-five inches high. Pearl du Monville was a midget. He was part French and part Hungarian, and maybe even part Bulgarian or somethin'. I can see him now, a sneer on his little pushed-in pan, swingin' a bamboo cane and smokin' a big cigar. He had a gray suit with a big black check into it, and he had a gray felt hat with one of them rainbow-colored hatbands onto it, like the young fellas wore in them days. He talked like he was talkin' into a tin can, but he didn't have no foreign accent. He might a been fifteen or he might a been a hundred, you couldn't tell. Pearl du Monville.

After the game with C'lumbus, Magrew headed straight for the Chittaden bar—the train for St. Louis wasn't goin' for three, four hours—and there he set, drinkin' rye and talkin' to this bartender.

"How I pity me, brother," Magrew was tellin' this bartender. "How I pity me." That was alwuz his favorite tune. So he was settin' there, tellin' this bartender how heartbreakin' it was to be manager of a bunch a blindfolded circus clowns, when up pops this Pearl du Monville outa nowheres.

It give Magrew the leapin' jumps. He thought at first maybe the D.T.'s had come back on him; he claimed he'd had 'em once, and little guys had popped up all around him, wearin' red, white and blue hats.

"Go on, now!" Magrew yells. "Get away from me!"

But the midget clumb up on a chair acrost the table from Magrew and says, "I seen that game today, Junior, and you ain't got no ball club. What you got there, Junior," he says, "is a side show."

"Whatta ya mean, 'Junior'?" says Magrew, touchin' the little guy to satisfy hisself he was real.

"Don't pay him no attention, mister," says the bartender. "Pearl calls everybody 'Junior,' 'cause it alwuz turns out he's a year older'n anybody else."

"Yeh?" says Magrew. "How old is he?"

"How old are you, Junior?" says the midget.

"Who, me? I'm fifty-three," says Magrew.

"Well, I'm fifty-four," says the midget.

Magrew grins and asts him what he'll have, and that was the beginnin' of their beautiful friendship, if you don't care what you say.

Pearl du Monville stood up on his chair and waved his cane around and pretended like he was ballyhooin' for a circus. "Right this way, folks!" he yells. "Come on in and see the greatest collection of freaks in the world! See the armless pitchers, see the eyeless batters, see the infielders with five thumbs!" and on and on like that, feedin' Magrew gall and handin' him a laugh at the same time, you might say.

You could hear him and Pearl du Monville hootin' and hollerin' and singin' way up to the fourth floor of the Chittaden, where the boys was packin' up. When it come time to go to the station, you can imagine how disgusted we was when we crowded into the doorway of that bar and seen them two singin' and goin' on.

"Well, well, well," says Magrew, lookin' up and spottin' us. "Look who's here. . . . Clowns, this is Pearl du Monville, a monseer of the old, old school. . . . Don't shake hands with 'em, Pearl, 'cause their fingers is made of chalk and would bust right off in your paws," he says, and he starts guffawin' and Pearl starts titterin' and we stand there givin' 'em the iron eye, it bein' the lowest ebb a ball-club manager'd got hisself down to since the national pastime was started.

Then the midget begun givin' us the ballyhoo. "Come on in!" he says, wavin' his cane. "See the legless base runners, see the outfielders with the butter fingers, see the southpaw with the arm of a little chee-ild!"

Then him and Magrew begun to hoop and holler and nudge each other till you'd of thought this little guy was the funniest guy than even Charlie Chaplin. The fellas filed outa the bar without a word and went on up to the Union Depot, leavin' me to handle Magrew and his new-found crony.

Well, I got 'em outa there finely. I had to take the little guy along, 'cause Magrew had a holt onto him like a vise and I couldn't pry him loose.

"He's comin' along as masket," says Magrew, holdin' the midget in the crouch of his arm like a football. And come along he did, hollerin' and protestin' and beatin' at Magrew with his little fists.

"Cut it out, will ya, Junior?" the little guy kept whinin'. "Come on, leave a man loose, will ya, Junior?"

But Junior kept a holt onto him and begun yellin', "See the guys with the glass arm, see the guys with the cast-iron brains, see the fielders with the feet on their wrists!"

So it goes, right through the whole Union Depot, with people starin' and catcallin', and he don't put the midget down till he gets him through the gates.

"How'm I goin' to go along without no toothbrush?" the midget asts. "What'm I goin' to do without no other suit?" he says.

"Doc here," says Magrew, meanin' me—"doc here will look after you like you was his own son, won't you, doc?"

I give him the iron eye, and he finely got on the train and prob'ly went to sleep with his clothes on.

This left me alone with the midget. "Lookit," I says to him. "Why don't you go on home now? Come mornin', Magrew'll forget all about you. He'll prob'ly think you was somethin' he seen in a nightmare maybe. And he ain't goin' to laugh so easy in the mornin', neither," I says. "So why don't you go on home?"

"Nix," he says to me. "Skiddoo," he says, "twenty-three for you," and he tosses his cane up into the vestibule of the coach and clam'ers on up after it like a cat. So that's the way Pearl du Monville come to go to St. Louis with the ball club.

I seen 'em first at breakfast the next day, settin' opposite each other; the midget playin' "Turkey in the Straw" on a harmonium and Magrew starin' at his eggs and bacon like they was a uncooked bird with its feathers still on.

"Remember where you found this?" I says, jerkin' my thumb at the midget. "Or maybe you think they come with breakfast on these trains," I says, bein' a good hand at turnin' a sharp remark in them days.

The midget puts down the harmonium and turns on me. "Sneeze," he says; "your brains is dusty." Then he snaps a couple of drops of water at me from a tumbler. "Drown," he says, tryin' to make his voice deep.

Now, both them cracks is Civil War cracks, but you'd of thought they was brand new and the funniest than any crack Magrew'd ever heard in his whole life. He started hoopin' and hollerin', and the midget started hoopin' and hollerin', so I walked on away and set down with Bugs Courtney and Hank Metters, payin' no attention to this weak-minded Damon and Phidias acrost the aisle.

Well, sir, the first game with St. Louis was rained out, and there we was facin' a double-header next day. Like maybe I told you, we lose the last three double-headers we play, makin' maybe twenty-five errors in the six games, which is all right for the intimates of a school for the blind, but is disgraceful for the world's champions. It was too wet to go to the zoo, and Magrew wouldn't let us go to the movies, 'cause they flickered so bad in them days. So we just set around, stewin' and frettin'.

One of the newspaper boys come over to take a pitture of Billy Klinger and Whitey Cott shakin' hands—this reporter'd heard about the fight—and whilst they was standin' there, toe to toe, shakin' hands, Billy give a back lunge and a jerk, and throwed Whitey over his shoulder into a corner of the room, like a sack a salt. Whitey come back at him with a chair, and Bethlehem broke loose in that there room. The camera was tromped to pieces like a berry basket. When we finely got 'em pulled apart, I heard a laugh, and there was Magrew and the midget standin' in the door and givin' us the iron eye.

"Wrasslers," says Magrew, cold-like, "that's what I got for a ball club, Mr. Du Monville, wrasslers—and not very good wrasslers at that, you ast me."

"A man can't be good at everythin'," says Pearl, "but he oughta be good at somethin'."

This sets Magrew guffawin' again, and away they go, the midget taggin' along by his side like a hound dog and handin' him a fast line of so-called comic cracks.

When we went out to face that battlin' St. Louis club in a double-header the next afternoon, the boys was jumpy as tin toys with keys in their back. We lose the first game, 7 to 2, and are trailin', 4 to 0, when the second game ain't but ten minutes old. Magrew set there like a stone statue, speakin' to nobody. Then, in their half a the fourth, somebody singled to center and knocked in two more runs for St. Louis.

That made Magrew squawk. "I wisht one thing," he says. "I wisht I was manager of a old ladies' sewin' circus 'stead of a ball club."

"You are, Junior, you are," says a familyer and disagreeable voice.

It was that Pearl du Monville again, poppin' up outa nowheres, swingin' his bamboo cane and smokin' a cigar that's three sizes too big for his face. By this time we'd finely got the other side out, and Hank Metters slithered a bat acrost the ground, and the midget had to jump to keep both his ankles from bein' broke.

I thought Magrew'd bust a blood vessel. "You hurt Pearl and I'll break your neck!" he yelled.

Hank muttered somethin' and went on up to the plate and struck out.

We managed to get a couple runs acrost in our half a the sixth, but they come back with three more in their half a the seventh, and this was too much for Magrew.

"Come on, Pearl," he says. "We're gettin' outa here."

"Where you think you're goin'?" I ast him.

"To the lawyer's again," he says cryptly.

159

"I didn't know you'd been to the lawyer's once, yet," I says.

"Which that goes to show how much you don't know," he says.

With that, they was gone, and I didn't see 'em the rest of the day, nor know what they was up to, which was a God's blessin'. We lose the nightcap, 9 to 3, and that puts us into second place plenty, and as low in our mind as a ball club can get.

The next day was a horrible day, like anybody that lived through it can tell you. Practice was just over and the St. Louis club was takin' the field, when I hears this strange sound from the stands. It sounds like the nervous whickerin' a horse gives when he smells somethin' funny on the wind. It was the fans ketchin' sight of Pearl du Monville, like you have prob'ly guessed. The midget had popped up onto the field all dressed up in a minacher club uniform, sox, cap, little letters sewed onto his chest, and all. He was swingin' a kid's bat and the only thing kept him from lookin' like a real ballplayer seen through the wrong end of a microscope was this cigar he was smokin'.

Bugs Courtney reached over and jerked it outa his mouth and throwed it away. "You're wearin' that suit on the playin' field," he says to him, severe as a judge. "You go insultin' it and I'll take you out to the zoo and feed you to the bears."

Pearl just blowed some smoke at him which he still has in his mouth.

Whilst Whitey was foulin' off four or five prior to strikin' out, I went on over to Magrew. "If I was as comic as you," I says, "I'd laugh myself to death," I says. "Is that any way to treat the uniform, makin' a mockery out of it?"

"It might surprise you to know I ain't makin' no mockery outa the uniform," says Magrew. "Pearl du Monville here has been made a bone-of-fida member of this so-called ball club. I fixed it up with the front office by long-distance phone."

"Yeh?" I says. "I can just hear Mr. Dillworth or Bart Jenkins agreein' to hire a midget for the ball club. I can just hear 'em." Mr. Dillworth was the owner of the club and Bart Jenkins was the secretary, and they never stood for no monkey business.

"May I be so bold as to inquire," I says, "just what you told 'em?"

"I told 'em," he says, "I wanted to sign up a guy they ain't no pitcher in the league can strike him out."

"Uh-huh," I says, "and did you tell 'em what size of a man he is?"

"Never mind about that," he says. "I got papers on me, made out legal and proper, constitutin' one Pearl du Monville a bone-of-fida member of this former ball club. Maybe that'll shame them big babies into gettin' in there and swingin', knowin' I can replace any one of 'em with a midget, if I have a mind to. A St. Louis lawyer I seen twice tells me it's all legal and proper."

"A St. Louis lawyer would," I says, "seein' nothin' could make him happier than havin' you makin' a mockery outa this one-time baseball outfit," I says.

Well, sir, it'll all be there in the papers of thirty, thirty-one year ago, and you could look it up. The game went along without no scorin' for seven innings, and since they ain't nothin' much to watch but guys poppin' up or strikin' out, the fans pay most of their attention to the goin's-on of Pearl du Monville. He's out there in front a the dugout, turnin' handsprings, balancin' his bat on his chin, walkin' a imaginary line, and so on. The fans clapped and laughed at him, and he ate it up.

So it went up to the last a the eighth, nothin' to nothin', not more'n seven, eight hits all told, and no errors on neither side. Our pitcher gets the first two men out easy in the eighth. Then up come a fella name of Porter or Billings, or some such name, and he lammed one up against the tobacco sign for three bases. The next guy up slapped the first ball out into left for a base hit, and in come the fella from third for the only run of the ball game so far. The crowd yelled, the look a death come onto Magrew's face again, and even the midget quit his tom-foolin'. Their next man fouled out back a third, and we come up for our last bats like a bunch a schoolgirls steppin' into a pool of cold water. I was lower in my mind than I'd been since the day in Nineteen-four when Chesbro throwed the wild pitch in the ninth inning with a man on third and lost the pennant for the Highlanders. I knowed something just as bad was goin' to happen, which shows I'm a clairvoyun, or was then.

When Gordy Mills hit out to second, I just closed my eyes. I opened 'em up again to see Dutch Muller standin' on second, dustin' off his pants, him havin' got his first hit in maybe twenty times to the plate. Next up was Harry Loesing, battin' for our pitcher, and he got a base on balls, walkin' on a fourth one you could a combed your hair with.

Then up come Whitey Cott, our lead-off man. He crotches down in what was prob'ly the most fearsome stanch in organized ball, but all he can do is pop out to short. That brung up Billy Klinger, with two down and a man on first and second. Billy took a cut at one you could a knocked a plug hat offa this here Carnera with it, but then he gets sense enough to wait 'em out, and finely he walks, too, fillin' the bases.

Yes, sir, there you are; the tyin' run on third and the winnin' run on second, first a the ninth, two men down, and Hank Metters comin' to the bat. Hank was built like a Pope-Hartford and he couldn't run no faster'n President Taft, but he had five home runs to his credit for the season, and that wasn't bad in them days. Hank was still hittin' better'n anybody else on the ball club, and it was mighty heartenin', seein' him stridin' up towards the plate. But he never got there.

"Wait a minute!" yells Magrew, jumpin' to his feet. "I'm sendin' in a pinch hitter!" he yells.

You could a heard a bomb drop. When a ball-club manager says he's sendin' in a pinch hitter for the best batter on the club, you know and I know and everybody knows he's lost his holt.

"They're goin' to be sendin' the funny wagon for you, if you don't watch out," I says, grabbin' a holt of his arm.

But he pulled away and run out towards the plate, yellin', "Du Monville battin' for Metters!"

All the fellas begun squawlin' at once, except Hank, and he just stood there starin' at Magrew like he'd gone crazy and was claimin' to be Ty Cobb's grandma or somethin'. Their pitcher stood out there with his hands on his hips and a disagreeable look on his face, and the plate umpire told Magrew to go on and get a batter up. Magrew told him again Du Monville was battin' for Metters, and the St. Louis manager finely got the idea. It brung him outa his dugout, howlin' and bawlin' like he'd lost a female dog and her seven pups.

Magrew pushed the midget towards the plate and he says to him, he says, "Just stand up there and hold that bat on your shoulder. They ain't a man in the world can throw three strikes in there 'fore he throws four balls!" he says.

"I get it, Junior!" says the midget. "He'll walk me and force in the tyin' run!" And he starts on up to the plate as cocky as if he was Willie Keeler.

I don't need to tell you Bethlehem broke loose on that there ball field. The fans got onto their hind legs, yellin' and whistlin', and everybody on the field begun wavin' their arms and hollerin' and shovin'. The plate umpire stalked over to Magrew like a traffic cop, waggin' his jaw and pointin' his finger, and the St. Louis manager kept yellin' like his house was on fire. When Pearl got up to the plate and stood there, the pitcher slammed his glove down onto the ground and started stompin' on it, and they ain't nobody can blame him. He's just walked two normal-sized human bein's, and now here's a guy up to the plate they ain't more'n twenty inches between his knees and his shoulders.

The plate umpire called in the field umpire, and they talked a while, like a couple doctors seein' the bucolic plague or somethin' for the first time. Then the plate umpire come over to Magrew with his arms folded acrost his chest, and he told him to go on and get a batter up, or he'd forfeit the game to St. Louis. He pulled out his watch, but somebody batted it outa his hand in the scufflin', and I thought there'd be a free-for-all, with everybody yellin' and shovin' except Pearl du Monville, who stood up at the plate with his little bat on his shoulder, not movin' a muscle.

163

Then Magrew played his ace. I seen him pull some papers outa his pocket and show 'em to the plate umpire. The umpire begun lookin' at 'em like they was bills for somethin' he not only never bought it, he never even heard of it. The other umpire studied 'em like they was a death warren, and all this time the St. Louis manager and the fans and the players is yellin' and hollerin'.

Well, sir, they fought about him bein' a midget, and they fought about him usin' a kid's bat, and they fought about where'd he been all season. They was eight or nine rule books brung out and everybody was thumbin' through 'em, tryin' to find out what it says about midgets, but it don't say nothin' about midgets, 'cause this was somethin' never'd come up in the history of the game before, and nobody'd ever dreamed about it, even when they has nightmares. Maybe you can't send no midgets in to bat nowadays, 'cause the old game's changed a lot, mostly for the worst, but you could then, it turned out.

The plate umpire finely decided the contrack papers was all legal and proper, like Magrew said, so he waved the St. Louis players back to their places and he pointed his finger at their manager and told him to quit hollerin' and get on back in the dugout. The manager says the game is percedin' under protest, and the umpire bawls, "Play ball!" over 'n' above the yellin' and booin', him havin' a voice like a hog-caller.

The St. Louis pitcher picked up his glove and beat at it with his fist six or eight times, and then got set on the mound and studied the situation. The fans realized he was really goin' to pitch to the midget, and they went crazy, hoopin' and hollerin' louder'n ever, and throwin' pop bottles and hats and cushions down onto the field. It took five, ten minutes to get the fans quieted down again, whilst our fellas that was on base set down on the bags and waited. And Pearl du Monville kept standin' up there with the bat on his shoulder, like he'd been told to.

So the pitcher starts studyin' the setup again, and you got to admit it was the strangest setup in a ball game since the players cut off their beards and begun wearin' gloves. I wisht I could call the pitcher's name—it wasn't old Barney Pelty nor Nig Jack Powell nor Harry Howell. He was a big right-hander, but I can't call his name. You could look it up. Even in a crotchin' position, the ketcher towers over the midget like the Washington Monument.

The plate umpire tries standin' on his tiptoes, then he tries crotchin' down, and he finely gets hisself into a stanch nobody'd ever seen on a ball field before, kinda squattin' down on his hanches.

Well, the pitcher is sore as a old buggy horse in fly time. He slams in the first pitch, hard and wild, and maybe two foot higher'n the midget's head.

"Ball one!" hollers the umpire over 'n' above the racket, 'cause everybody is yellin' worsten ever.

The ketcher goes on out towards the mound and talks to the pitcher and hands him the ball. This time the big right-hander tried a undershoot, and it comes in a little closer, maybe no higher'n a foot, foot and a half above Pearl's head. It would a been a strike with a human bein' in there, but the umpire's got to call it, and he does.

"Ball two!" he bellers.

The ketcher walks on out to the mound again, and the whole infield comes over and gives advice to the pitcher about what they'd do in a case like this, with two balls and no strikes on a batter that oughta be in a bottle of alcohol 'stead of up there at the plate in a big-league game between the teams that is fightin' for first place.

For the third pitch, the pitcher stands there flatfooted and tosses up the ball like he's playin' ketch with a little girl.

Pearl stands there motionless as a hitchin' post, and the ball comes in big and slow and high—high for Pearl, that is, it bein' about on a level with his eyes, or a little higher'n a grown man's knees.

They ain't nothin' else for the umpire to do, so he calls, "Ball three!"

Everybody is onto their feet, hoopin' and hollerin', as the pitcher sets to throw ball four. The St. Louis manager is makin' signs and faces like he was a contorturer, and the infield is givin' the pitcher some more advice about what to do this time. Our boys who was on base stick right onto the bag, runnin' no risk of bein' nipped for the last out.

Well, the pitcher decides to give him a toss again, seein' he come closer with that than with a fast ball. They ain't nobody ever seen a slower ball throwed. It come in big as a balloon and slower'n any ball ever throwed before in the major leagues. It come right in over the plate in front of Pearl's chest, lookin' prob'ly big as a full moon to Pearl. They ain't never been a minute like the minute that followed since the United States was founded by the Pilgrim grandfathers.

Pearl du Monville took a cut at that ball, and he hit it! Magrew give a groan like a poleaxed steer as the ball rolls out in front a the plate into fair territory.

"Fair ball!" yells the umpire, and the midget starts runnin' for first, still carryin' that little bat, and makin' maybe ninety foot an hour. Bethlehem breaks loose on that ball field and in them stands. They ain't never been nothin' like it since creation was begun.

The ball's rollin' slow, on down towards third, goin' maybe eight, ten foot. The infield comes in fast and our boys break from their bases like hares in a brush fire. Everybody is standin' up, yellin' and hollerin', and Magrew is tearin' his hair outa his head, and the midget is scamperin' for first with all the speed of one of them little dashhounds carryin' a satchel in his mouth.

The ketcher gets to the ball first, but he boots it on out past the pitcher's box, the pitcher fallin' on his face tryin' to stop it, the shortstop sprawlin' after it full length and zaggin' it on over towards the second baseman, whilst Muller is scorin' with the tyin' run and Loesing is roundin' third with the winnin' run. Ty Cobb could a made a three-bagger outa that bunt, with everybody fallin' over theirself tryin' to pick the ball up. But Pearl is still maybe fifteen, twenty feet from the bag, toddlin' like a baby and yeepin' like a trapped rabbit, when the second baseman finely gets a holt of that ball and slams it over to first. The first baseman ketches it and stomps on the bag, the base umpire waves Pearl out, and there goes your old ball game, the craziest ball game ever played in the history of the organized world.

Their players start runnin' in, and then I see Magrew. He starts after Pearl, runnin' faster'n any man ever run before. Pearl sees him comin' and runs behind the base umpire's legs and gets a holt onto 'em. Magrew comes up, pantin' and roarin', and him and the midget plays ring-around-a-rosy with the umpire, who keeps shovin' at Magrew with one hand and tryin' to slap the midget loose from his legs with the other.

Finely Magrew ketches the midget, who is still yeepin' like a stuck sheep. He gets holt of that little guy by both his ankles and starts whirlin' him round and round his head like Magrew was a hammer thrower and Pearl was the hammer. Nobody can stop him without gettin' their head knocked off, so everybody just stands there and yells. Then Magrew lets the midget fly. He flies on out towards second, high and fast, like a human home run, headed for the soap sign in center field.

Their shortstop tries to get to him, but he can't make it, and I knowed the little fella was goin' to bust to pieces like a dollar watch on a asphalt street when he hit the ground. But it so happens their center fielder is just crossin' second, and he starts runnin' back, tryin' to get under the midget, who had took to spiralin' like a football 'stead of turnin' head over foot, which give him more speed and more distance.

I know you never seen a midget ketched, and you prob'ly never even seen one throwed. To ketch a midget that's been throwed by a heavy-muscled man and is flyin' through the air, you got to run under him and with him and pull your hands and arms back and down when you ketch him, to break the compact of his body, or you'll bust him in two like a matchstick. I seen Bill Lange and Willie Keeler and Tris Speaker make some wonderful ketches in my day, but I never seen nothin' like that center fielder. He goes back and back and still further back and he pulls that midget down outa the air like he was liftin' a sleepin' baby from a cradle. They wasn't a bruise onto him, only his face was the color of cat's meat and he ain't got no air in his chest. In his excitement, the base umpire, who was runnin' back with the center fielder when he ketched Pearl, yells, "Out!" and that give hysteries to the Bethlehem which was ragin' like Niagry on that ball field.

Everybody was hoopin' and hollerin' and yellin' and runnin', with the fans swarmin' onto the field, and the cops tryin' to keep order, and some guys laughin' and some of the women fans cryin', and six or eight of us holdin' onto Magrew to keep him from gettin' at that midget and finishin' him off. Some of the fans picks up the St. Louis pitcher and the center fielder, and starts carryin' 'em around on their shoulders, and they was the craziest goin's-on knowed to the history of organized ball on this side of the 'Lantic Ocean.

I seen Pearl du Monville strugglin' in the arms of a lady fan with a ample bosom, who was laughin' and cryin' at the same time, and him beatin' at her with his little fists and bawlin' and yellin'. He clawed his way loose finely and disappeared in the forest of legs which made that ball field look like it was Coney Island on a hot summer's day.

That was the last I ever seen of Pearl du Monville. I never seen hide nor hair of him from that day to this, and neither did no-body else. He just vanished into the thin of the air, as the fella says. He was ketched for the final out of the ball game and that was the end of him, just like it was the end of the ball game, you might say, and also the end of our losin' streak, like I'm goin' to tell you.

That night we piled onto a train for Chicago, but we wasn't snarlin' and snappin' any more. No, sir, the ice was finely broke and a new spirit come into that ball club. The old zip come back with the disappearance of Pearl du Monville out back a second base. We got to laughin' and talkin' and kiddin' together, and 'fore long Magrew was laughin' with us. He got a human look onto his pan again, and he quit whinin' and complainin' and wishtin' he was in heaven with the angels.

Well, sir, we wiped up that Chicago series, winnin' all four games, and makin' seventeen hits in one of 'em. Funny thing was, St. Louis was so shook up by that last game with us, they never did hit their stride again. Their center fielder took to misjudgin' everything that come his way, and the rest a the fellas followed suit, the way a club'll do when one guy blows up.

'Fore we left Chicago, I and some of the fellas went out and bought a pair of them little baby shoes, which we had 'em golded over and give 'em to Magrew for a souvenir, and he took it all in good spirit. Whitey Cott and Billy Klinger made up and was fast friends again, and we hit our home lot like a ton of dynamite and they was nothin' could stop us from then on.

I don't recollect things as clear as I did thirty, forty year ago. I can't read no fine print no more, and the only person I got to check with on the golden days of the national pastime, as the fella says, is my friend, old Milt Kline, over in Springfield, and his mind ain't as strong as it once was.

He gets Rube Waddell mixed up with Rube Marquard, for one thing, and anybody does that oughta be put away where he won't bother nobody. So I can't tell you the exact margin we win the pennant by. Maybe it was two and a half games, or maybe it was three and a half. But it'll all be there in the newspapers and record books of thirty, thirty-one year ago and, like I was sayin', you could look it up.

Both "Haircut" and the Thurber story work primarily because both writers, perhaps having learned something from Mark Twain, perhaps serendipitously having reinvented the innocently deadpan delivery that Twain employed so magically to lure his readers into snares where he could tickle them to death, never falter in their confidence that the reader's intelligence is equal to the demands they make upon it (Edmund Wilson, reviewing Lardner's 1924 collection, *How to Write Short Stories,* took the critic's option most infuriating to the writer, chiding him for not having written a different kind of book: he condescendingly made his suspicions pretty clear when he asked whether Lardner would "go on to his *Huckleberry Finn* or has . . . already told all he knows," describing him as another "man who has the freedom of the modern West no less than Mark Twain did of the old one, who approaches it, as Mark Twain did, with a perceptive interest in human beings instead of with the naturalist's formula. . . .").

Lardner's barber and Thurber's trainer, it needs noting here, represent sterling exemplars of triumphant employment of one of the trickiest story-telling devices available: the obtuse narrator. That is why I enlist them here instead of, say, Twain's Huck Finn. Huck was unlettered and unpolished, but he was not obtuse; since Twain was careful not to couch Huck's insights in the diction of a man of the world—in other words, Twain's own—but to have them issue in the form of speech that a bright but unlettered country lad would use, he was at liberty to allow Huck to deliver then-decidedly-unpopular judgments about racial matters without jarring the reader.

Lardner and Thurber took on tougher jobs. Their storytellers were stupid in their own right. The writer who elects to tell his story through the mouth of a dimwit must somehow contrive to convey all of the data that the reader needs to develop his own judgment of the characters in the story, without exceeding the plain limit of the dullard's powers of observation. And he must convey those ostensibly casual and fortuitous perceptions without once causing the garrulous dolt to utter a syllable betraying a glimmer of intelligence sufficient to suggest that he is putting something over on the reader. By the choice of that device, the scribbler limits himself to reporting solely those facts and incidents that the stupid narrator would ordinarily have witnessed, or heard about, in the normal course of days that seem to him to have been perfectly routine and unexceptionable. So he must know and tell everything that the reader ought to know, while understanding the implications of none of it, serving as a human version of the tireless video surveillance cameras that banks install to monitor mundane transaction after mundane transaction against the possibility that something extraordinary—a holdup—will occur, deserving preservation. To the reader it must appear that that dim bulb was merely lucky and happened to be present when a remarkable event occurred. The writer needs a great deal of critical acumen when he draws such a narrator, precisely because the character can display none himself.

I think that chore is harder for the writer working toward the end of the twentieth century than it was for Lardner and Thurber. They had a blanket license to employ orthographic dialect—phonetic spelling, e.g., "theayter" for "theater"; "aw de cologne" for "eau de cologne"—as a device to supplement busted syntax—"I got another barber" instead of "I've got another barber"; "You must of" instead of "You must have" (I happen to think "you must of" unnecessarily jostles today's reader's eye, even though O'Hara employed it sedulously—what the speaker means to say is almost certainly "must've," and I don't see why he shouldn't be tacitly *and* typographically forgiven his poor elocution). One seldom encounters such excesses now, which leads me to suspect that if they are being committed, and then submitted, editors are rejecting them.

If you would like to see why editors would behave in such high-handed fashion, undergoing an excruciating demonstration of my reason for suspecting that orthographic dialect is no longer welcome in large doses, make another trip to your library and borrow—for God's sake, don't buy the thing; this is one book you'll return well before the date due, and be more than pleased to do so—*Old Creole Days,* a collection of stories by George Washington Cable, set in New Orleans and foisted on a defenseless public in 1879, or any of his novels similarly set and made equally unbearable by Cable's unrelenting insistence on phonetic spelling of a drawl that is music to hear but gibberish to see. If you prefer to save yourself the library outing and take it on faith: today's N'Awlins longtime dweller alludes to his newspaper as "th' Tahms-Pikune" (at least that's what it sounds like to these foreign ears from Boston); now imagine not just a sentence or two, or a mere page or so, but a whole damned book stuffed to the eaves with such visual atrocities, demanding that the mind desiring story first earn needed data by translating every line. An appalling prospect: we ain't got time furrit.

Therefore, think of orthographic dialect as careful chefs think of garlic: something to be used sparingly, to enhance without overpowering the effect intended, and always with due attention to the comfort of those later to consume the handiwork. My characters occasionally refer to the Boston entry in the National Hockey League as "da Broons," because that is the locution now commonly, though by no means universally, employed by Bostonians of disparate social classes to enunciate "The Bruins." It percolated up from the blue-collar set and is now indulged through clenched teeth by the higher orders afflicted by Harvard-Wellesley lockjaw, in order to demonstrate that they too are regular chaps. This is comical behavior, but the amusement is not the sort intended; the usage serves to establish conclusively that they are not regular chaps at all but irredeemably and unjustifiably condescending snobs.

There isn't any bright-line rule to be laid down here or anywhere else for ready reference when you are not sure whether an impatient and distracted receptionist should be quoted as saying: "That's what you asked me for, idnit?" instead of: "That's what you asked me for, isn't it?" In the absence of such a rule, I recommend that you establish a general policy: don't do it too often. If you think you may have done it enough, don't do it any more for a while. If any doubt lingers, prefer the conventional spelling. True art is knowing when to stop, idnit? And that last indulgence of mine constitutes a clear case of policy violation.

Given that shift of taste, it could be argued that John P. Marquand (1893–1960) is for today's developing writer a better guide for mastery of the obtuse-narrator mode. Quite as unjustly neglected as O'Hara in the current canon of modern American literature—though their contemporaries did treat Marquand somewhat better; he won the 1937 Pulitzer Prize for fiction—Marquand in his serious efforts was the very model of the modulated gentleman. The reason that *all* of his work, including his best, is relegated to the bins of disregard is obvious in his case (as it is not in O'Hara's): While both prospered mightily for four decades as purveyors by appointment of short fiction to popular magazines, O'Hara, from the standpoint of literary respectability, chose his chief outlet—*The New Yorker*—more felicitously (not that it did him any good, once the checks were cashed). Marquand, though privately regretting the subordination of his prestige to prosperity, cranked out such pedestrian stories as those of his Japanese detective, Mr. Moto, almost as industriously as his buyers at the resolutely middlebrow *Saturday Evening Post* exhorted him to do, all but forfeiting, in the process of defraying the ruinous expenses of his habit of making bad marriages, and worse divorces, his claim for respect as an artist, both publicly and in his own estimation (Millicent Bell's superb *Marquand: An American Life,* 1979, affectingly documents his chagrin at his own conduct).

Such popular attitudes permeate the consciousness of the writer's time and penetrate the minds of those who grow up during it. The teachers who began their ascent to influential positions after World War II, and thus participated in the gradual development of the consensus about what merited inclusion in the modern American literary repertoire, certainly recognized Marquand's name (if it was ever mentioned) as a performer of some reputation on the pages of the slicks they saw in their homes and barbershops, and probably should not be blamed for giving short shrift to his actual honest work.

Today's aspiring writers, though, can uncritically accept that implied permission to ignore Marquand's good work only at cost to themselves, especially if they wish to write effective satire, a term that lately has suffered a connotative shift that requires corrective digression here before we proceed with an excerpt from Marquand.

The first—and therefore preferred—meaning of satire recorded in the 1987 Second Edition of the Random House *Dictionary of the English Language* is: "the use of irony, sarcasm, ridicule, or the like, in exposing, denouncing, or deriding, vice, folly, etc." Not until you reach the second definition is "scorn" offered as a synonym; "burlesque," "caricature," "travesty" and "lampoon" follow well after that, but those are the senses in which the word is most commonly used today.

What we have here is evidence of a lexical shift, very likely attributable to the indiscriminate and habitual use of *satire* as journalistic and critical shorthand designating something written or performed that first invites the reader or viewer to experience the corrosive contempt that the writer feels for the obvious (real) target of his pen, and then enthusiastically proselytizes the previously neutral reader or viewer to join in its noisy proclamation. It amounts to secular preaching, ideological evangelism on whatever subject—racism; sexism; nuclear power; nuclear war; air pollution—happens to be most fashionable, conducted by that branch of the thought police that happens to have gained temporary prominence among the contending gangs.

Superficially the usage seems meet and just. The more articulate of professed modern satirists regularly claim Jonathan Swift as their spiritual forefather, and he was not only a frocked preacher by trade but also a secular scourge and common scold by avocation. But trouble begins with the inability of his would-be heirs to see that they and their siblings, whether posturing and mugging on NBC's "Saturday Night Live," and "David Letterman," or in theaters mistaking the flinging of feces for rapier thrusts of wit, are disregarding, first, the fact that Swift was a genius, able to get away with stuff that lesser mortals bungle, and, secondly, that their eighteenth-century mentor did not depend for success in his sardonic forays on popularity in the commercial marketplace. They of the twentieth do. Salaried entertainers with airtime to fill enjoy the option to flay villains of their own choosing only so long as they are careful to match those choices to those of their predictable audiences. Free-lance writers confront a less attractive prospect.

Books and dramatic productions alike require today investment of large amounts of money as preconditions of existence. Seldom are publishers sufficiently inflamed by broad farce to finance its appearance in printed form. And Broadway money angels have embroidered on their cuffs the irrefutable maxim that "satire is what closes Saturday night" (after fewer than seven performances). There are only two varieties of potential customers for books and plays that attack and deride some prominent person or movement: those who share the scornful artist's point of view and will pay money for the privilege of sitting in the choir while he preaches it, and those who, though they do not share it, will pay money to have it preached to them. Separately or in combination, those two groups are seldom numerous enough to defray modern costs of production. The author is therefore faced with the dilemma of whether to preserve the white-hot integrity of his iconoclastic screed (which means he will most likely never see it published or performed) or to water down his message to the point at which it becomes palatable to a large body of consumers (and usually ceases to be satire, because it is only mocking, not exposing, follies already perceived and jeered by the chic to whom it appeals).

Consequently, when the mass media inform us that a contemporary American writer has managed to create a successful piece of satire, we can reliably infer not only that it meets the strict definition of *satire*—employing irony to expose folly or stupidity—but that it is not a disguised tract. In other words, it does not call for complicity of reader or audience in the humiliation of its characters as the price of admission to its delights. When that rare event seems to have occurred, punctilious critics usually signal the sighting by describing the work as "gentle satire," in the hope of alerting the sensitive prospective consumer to the arrival of something refreshingly different from the usual strident propaganda merchandised as *satire*.

I suppose this is serviceable enough, as far as it goes, so long as it functions in fact to convey the underlying appeal of the work: its author has rested content to have created a fiction that amuses the reader into the discovery of the actual silliness of a reality he had not previously fully understood. Behavior which had theretofore seemed to him perfectly harmless, if he noticed it at all, under the writer's scrutiny now stands revealed as the folly, recklessness, stupidity, or wickedness that it really is. The author has not importuned the reader to take up a cudgel, storm any battlement, or overthrow the government by force and violence as evidence of *bona fides* in delivery of applause and loud hosannas of thanksgiving for his great fortune in living at the same time as this messianic scribbler. The reader does not even have to sign a petition demanding an immediate end be made of the persons or institutions which have provoked the author to produce this masterpiece. All he has to do is see something he had not seen before, and if that sight makes him think differently than he had thought before, well, for the self-effacing writer that is reward enough.

All of which is a long and irritated way of explaining that no single piece of writing should be expected to produce more than one catharsis or epiphany per author-reader transaction, and that moment of new insight and perception into the human condition should be the reader's to enjoy, not the writer's to exploit.

That brings us to *The Late George Apley,* surely "gentle satire" in the present dispensation, but also a durable and remarkable work of careful fiction. Its premise is that birth into the genteel, prosperous, Brahmin society of late nineteenth- and early twentieth-century Boston and the North Shore conferred only revocable entitlements to enjoyment of its advantages. Training of the sons and daughters of the better families commenced virtually, if subtly, at birth, and continued well into their adult lives, featuring as many sharp snubbings of their leashes and withdrawals of their privileges as might be required to bring them docilely to heel. This discipline continued until they had either obediently foreclosed to themselves all avenues of unacceptable conduct, or had by parenthood become unwitting collaborators in the preservation of the same system that had housebroken them. It is unusual for a practicing mentor to question the validity of the very code he is enforcing upon a defenseless someone else, reflexively inculcating the same strictures that made him what he is.

That is not a thesis of much shock potential now, and it was not when Marquand appropriated it for his *Apley* theme. The Society of Jesus has for centuries placidly acceded to the accusation that their *ratio studiorum* is bottomed on the confidence that a boy given into their care and supervision by the age of seven will be theirs for life. The novel did not beguile the readers of the thirties because it reported late-breaking news; it interested them because Marquand made them see afresh what happens to a rather ordinary man who is systematically thwarted every time he manifests even the most tentative inclination to exercise his own will in the accomplishment of his own preferences. There was nothing morally or legally wrong with his first real love; she was merely unacceptable because she was of Irish Catholic descent and came from Central Square in Cambridge, instead of being Yankee Protestant and born of worthy stock wintering on Beacon Hill and summering at Marblehead. There was nothing reprehensible in Apley's impulse to improve the lot of the employees of the Apley textile mills, but it withered under the cold judgment of his elders, who feared that its indulgence might in the long run foment a revolution of rising expectations, and who could say where that might end? George Apley was not a courageous man. He did suffer from occasional temptations to commit spontaneous acts that his overseers thought unseemly, and he sometimes resisted fresh and boring obligations broached as opportunities. But not for very long; he was a dutiful and docile man.

Marquand was no fool. George Apley's life, and the real lives that it aped from the real lives of the people that Marquand saw around him (he was born in Wilmington, Delaware, but spent his formative years in the midst of Apley's sort of people, on the ground that they all trod, and he was a bright, alert lad), lacked dramatic impact. Successful novels require tension, either major hazard to, or recurring minor jeopardy of, the character or his principles, so that the reader can vicariously root for him in the ecstasy of victory or sorrow in the final agony of defeat.

Marquand, having brought to the boiling a good many slick pots for the *Saturday Evening Post,* was too much the practiced professional to ignore the probability that a reader who is proffered an unvarnished tale of a boring life would dismiss its mere narration as a boring novel and banish all temptation to acquire the weary thing, let alone read through it. He therefore conscripted Willing, as close to having been one of the deceased George Apley's trusted friends as Apley and his social code allowed such intimacies, and put *him* in jeopardy of self-discovery and dismay.

Willing is commissioned by Apley's son, John, a young man still resisting the commands of Apley's code, to write a biography of his father. John has an ulterior motive: he wants the whole truth told, so that any reader with an ounce of common sense will perceive at once how his father had his better nature suffocated out of him, and thus perhaps infer the motive underlying John's rebarbative reaction to his father's identical treatment of himself. Willing proves not entirely eponymous when it comes to execution of John's stated purpose; Willing is himself another sere product of the Brahmin desiccation process, and as good slaves often do, has come to love his chains. If he portrays George Apley as the victim of his upbringing, he will be depicting himself equally as victim, and, by implication, repudiating what he has learned he must hold dear.

Chapter 12 neatly conveys Willing's mounting uneasiness, as he strives manfully to present a cheerful countenance to a perfectly grim situation. Apley, cleansed of his unfortunate infatuation for the Irish girl, has surrendered to propriety and married acceptably, taking Catherine Bosworth in Brahmin cold-roast wedlock at the Arlington Street (Unitarian-Universalist) Church in Boston. This is Willing's ruminative retrospective on the whole event.

MARRIAGE

Circumstances Surrounding an Important Step in a Well-Rounded Life

Though Apley was a "man's man," he was soon to become very satisfactorily a woman's man as well. The emotions and upsets of courtship, so characteristic of certain undisciplined elements in other sections of the country, are, fortunately, no part of our best tradition. Here, marriage has always been taken in the stride of life, as a sacrament to be entered into soberly, cheerfully and irrevocably. In February, 1890, Mr. and Mrs. James Bosworth announced the engagement of George Apley to their daughter, Catharine—in every way an eminently suitable match, not only from the point of view of property but, more important still, from a community of healthy tastes and tradition. These two had played together in childhood and had trod the same paths of youth with a similarity of upbringing which could not but make them congenial. The Bosworths, who could boast among their ancestors James Bosworth of the Assistants' Court in Massachusetts and Ephraim Bosworth, a ringleader in the Boston Tea Party, joined the Apleys in expressing their pleasure in the approaching union.

Letter from Mrs. James Bosworth to George Apley

My dear George:

Catharine to-day told me her great news in the sweetest way, that we were to lose a daughter but were to gain a son. Of course, when she spoke of losing a daughter this was a most complete jest. Neither her father nor I would possibly tolerate losing what we hold more dear than life itself. It simply means that you will now become a member of our family and join our happy circle. James is already arranging to have the old barn at Mulberry Beach made into a very sweet little cottage, so that you and Catharine can start your life this summer only a stone's throw from us.

We must both insist on this. I know you will understand, because you are your own dear mother's son and must have her own sensibility, that Catharine, though she seems robust, is actually very sensitive and is wholly dependent upon her parents. I know that you will not think of separating any of us, and that is why James and I are both so pleased. . . .

Letter to George Apley from James Bosworth

Dear George:

I am still somewhat shaken by our last interview, as my love for Catharine transcends my love for anything else. My worst fears are allayed by your assurance that we would never be separated by any greater distance than the suburban limits. Our business talk, coupled with a letter from your father, has been eminently satisfactory. It is our joint wish to have you two start life comfortably, but simply, and I feel that we can make the necessary arrangement. . . .

AMONG THE OTHER LETTERS received by George Apley from his family and his warm friends, all of them expressing the pleasure so natural for such a felicitous and suitable occasion, it is fortunate that we have the wishes of his father. It appears that Thomas Apley was in New York at the time, where he was detained, as seems to have been so frequently the case in those years, by business negotiations.

Dear George:

Your letter reached me at the Park Avenue Hotel this morning as I started down to Wall Street. I only wish I were out of the confusion of this place to tell you at first hand the happiness and relief which I must now set down on paper. I have always had a feeling that the Apley stock is solid at bottom. We may sow our wild oats, — I was young myself once, — but now, thank God, we are out of the woods.

Catharine, whom I am looking forward to greeting as my daughter, has always seemed to me a very noble girl and her position and yours in the scheme of things are such that there will be none of the frictions due to divergent backgrounds, which might occur for instance in a New York and Boston union. You have shown the good sense, too, to realize that beauty is only skin deep and that there are more important elements in the holy bond of matrimony.

The income from the little which your grandmother has left you, which is now invested in sound railroad bonds; except for a few thousand dollars which I used some years ago for taking a "flier" in telephone stock and which I will make up to you in case this invention eventually becomes only a fad, should be enough for you to start a modest establishment. In addition to this, I shall continue at least a portion of my allowance to you.

This, unless my belief is wrong in Catharine's sagacity as a housekeeper, will be enough to keep the wolf from the door. Mr. Bosworth has told me that he plans to do the barn over for you at his summer place. It happens that I was obliged only the other day to foreclose a mortgage on a small dwelling house in Gloucester Street. This was one of a parcel of three. As I have already turned the other two over at a profit, I have nearly cleared this one house on the transaction, and I shall turn it over to you as a wedding gift. In order that things may not come too easily, however, I am putting a small mortgage on it, which your Uncle William has kindly consented to hold, and you must be responsible for the interest.

The time is coming also when you must be launched in business, and I shall talk to you soon about a suitable law office for you to enter. I am very glad to hear from several older men that you are generally well thought of, and that shortly your name will come up for the Province Club. There will, of course, be no difficulty here, particularly if you separate yourself a little more from the amiable nonsense of the Berkley Club.

There have been some very disturbing rumours lately that a small group of hare-brained meddlers is agitating to have the Charles River dammed, so that the flats of the rear of our house on Beacon Street, which I have always enjoyed watching at low tide, will be covered at all times. This is only another example of the constant inroads being made upon the rights of individuals who have had the good sense to amass a small amount of property. Something must be done to stop this at once, but I shall talk to you about this on my return. . . .

THE LAST PARAGRAPH of this letter, referring to the project of the Charles River Basin, now a veritable jewel of water resting on the bosom of our city, may seem curious in the light of the present. It was to play a significant and somewhat sad part in the life of George Apley, as we shall see in a later chapter.

Now, however, we continue on a more happy strain and quote a letter from Elizabeth Apley to the bride-to-be: —

My darling, darling Catharine:

My own dear George himself told his first love, his mother, his tender news this very morning. He told it in such a manly way, so simply and so sweetly, that I wish you could have been there to have heard him. He came up to me at the front window, as I was holding a bit of burning tobacco leaf in a dustpan to kill the aphids that have attacked my dear geraniums, and he said: "Mother, I think you will be glad to know that Catharine Bosworth has consented to be my wife." Of course, the first thing I did, dear Catharine (and would not any woman do the same?), was to give way to a few tears, as I thought of this impending change in my dear boy's life — but they were most of them tears of gladness. The rest, let me hasten to add, were foolish tears betraying the weakness of a fond parent who feels that her nest is being broken up and that her brood of dear ones is flying from her. But then, as my dear Georgie brought me a glass of water, I remembered, as I hope you will, that Georgie hates tears and I knew how foolish I was. I had only to say to myself that I was not losing a son but was gaining a dear, sweet daughter — how sweet I think I know. Indeed, I know very well that you will never take my Georgie from me, for nothing can sever the love of a mother for her son. I know that you will let Georgie and me have as many friendly, playful chats as we ever had before. I know that you will realize as well as I do that George is a dear, sensitive boy who needs a mother's understanding. I know that you must love the same things in George that I love and we two will share that love together. Darling, darling Catharine, will you come to me this afternoon so that we may have a quiet and intimate little talk? There are so many things that I can tell you about dear George. . . .

THIS INTEREST IN and this solicitude for the welfare of George Apley forms the theme of letters from many other relatives, since the position of both the Apley and the Bosworth families was such as to render the approaching union one of extraordinary significance. That friendly concern for the affairs of others which so characterizes our society gave rise to inevitable speculation as to the future happiness of the fortunate young couple. The devotion of Catharine Bosworth's father on the one hand and of George Apley's mother on the other received a particular and deserved meed of praise from all who knew them. Thus the correspondence nearly all deals at length with efforts to make George Apley understand the sacrifices of these two parents. The letter of his Uncle Horatio Brent is almost the only one which sounds a slightly different note.

Dear George:

I must congratulate you on marrying Catharine Bosworth but I wonder whether you know exactly what marriage means. It is, my boy, a damnably serious business, particularly around Boston. Remember, George, that you not only marry a wife but also your wife's entire family. Much as you may love your wife, it is hard even with all the good will in the world suddenly to love the whole new group of extraneous people who fall your way, simply because they are relatives of your wife. You're fortunate in that you know most of these people already but you are going to know them differently now. I'm afraid you're going to find it a little hard to love old Bosworth. I know I never did, but don't let me discourage you.

What bothers me most is that I am afraid you don't know much about women. I didn't when I married your aunt, but I know a great deal now and I have been around a bit in my time. I think it might be a very useful thing if you were to have lunch with me at the Club and let me give you a few bits of advice which are not printed ordinarily in books. I feel sure you'll need it later. Personally, I never became so seriously interested in sport as I did after I was married. By this autumn you may want to go with me down to Carolina for the quail shooting and next spring we must go up to Muskeg River where I have salmon rights. The great thing about marriage is not to think too much about it. Your affectionate uncle, . . .

IT IS THE WRITER'S BELIEF that nearly any man must look back to this important period in his life with somewhat mingled emotions, in that the new social contacts and this new and beautiful relationship cannot but cause a certain amount of mental confusion. The excitement resultant from the preparations for the event probably explains why the bridegroom is so frequently an abject and harassed object by the time he finally approaches the altar. It explains, too, the reason for many unfortunate crises. Thus the writer can recall, without mentioning names, as indeed many others also must recall who read these pages, several persons with the very best background who have disappeared from Boston on the eve of matrimony. Most of these have re-established their position at some time later, but two, to the writer's certain knowledge, have never been heard of since; and it may be added that their names are now never mentioned by their relatives. Though George Apley was of a different stamp, he revealed something of the turbulent uncertainty which has beset so many in a letter to his intimate friend Winthrop Vassal.

Dear Winty:

Thanks for your note about Catharine. I know that I am very, very fortunate because I don't know what she sees in me. She is so vastly finer in every way than I am, more generous, more intelligent and a great deal more sensitive. There is one thing about her I did not know until after we were engaged. For several years Catharine has been collecting butter knives, and she now has one of the best collections in the country. That is quite remarkable, isn't it? What with preparations for our house in the country, and what with wedding presents coming in, and what with everyone being so kind and anxious to help — there cannot be kinder people in the world than those in Boston — I don't know exactly where I am or what I am doing. Everyone wants to give us tea parties and dinners. My Uncle William has already sent his wedding present, a fourteenth-century tapestry; it must be put somewhere where he will see it, but I don't know where. Uncle Horatio has sent me a pair of Irish setters and I don't know where I am going to keep them either, particularly as it appears that Catharine doesn't like dogs. Aunt Hancock has sent me a dining-room table, and so it goes. Marriage is a very serious business, Winty. Catharine has set the seventeenth of June for the wedding. What frightens me more than anything else is that I may never see my old friends again. We must all stay together,

Winty, things must be the same between us. You and Mike and Chick and I and the old crowd at the Club mustn't drift apart. . . .

THIS PREOCCUPATION of George Apley, not indeed unusual to one who is embarking on a new and untried stage of existence, that the friends of his own incarnation might be leaving him, should have been very quickly dissipated by the loyalty of these same friends at numerous small dinners which they gave him in the interval between his engagement and his marriage in early June. Nevertheless, though Apley was fully aware, as he often said himself, that he was the happiest man in the world, he often gave way on such occasions to a strain of sentimental sadness. This was particularly true at his own bachelor's dinner, attended of course by the ushers, among whom the present writer, his old friends, Chickering, Walker, and Vassal, and several of his contemporary cousins were numbered. The writer remembers this occasion very well indeed. Though not unlike many others which he has attended, the group around the table was of the best. With such people around the board, all from very much the same section of life and each known so well to the other, there was no need for anyone to display the care or reticence which his caution and sense of fitness might have demanded of him at another time and place. The atmosphere in the private dining-room of the Parker House was one of a complete and unalloyed friendship as course followed course. Thomas Apley, sensing the importance of this dinner, had sent over a half-dozen Madeira which had been to Charleston and back in ballast fifty years before, and had instructed the management to serve unlimited champagne. Vassal told several of his inimitable stories and Walker sang songs in his fine baritone until everyone in the room, including the waiters, joined the chorus. Then there followed a round of toasts, one given by the writer himself. It was noticed at the time that Apley seemed distrait, but no more so than might be expected, until the company, each placing a foot upon the table, sang "Should auld acquaintance be forgot . . . ?" — at which point Apley actually gave way to tears. This sign of emotion was received with hearty applause, marred only by a display of carelessness on the part of one of the guests, who stepped out of a window. The dining-room, fortunately, was on the second story, so that a broken arm and two shattered front teeth were the only results of an accident that might have cast a gloom on the whole company.

The wedding, which was solemnized behind the brownstone façade of the Arlington Street Church, was, as has already been said, an occasion of importance. The agitation of George Apley, as he waited in the small cloakroom, could readily be explained if one took a glimpse at the pews of that great edifice. Like many another happy bridegroom, he was pale and perspired freely, and several of his remarks may be quoted as completely characteristic of one in his position.

"Good God," he said, "is everyone in the world here?" Shortly afterwards he said in a spirit of pure facetiousness: "Perhaps Catharine has backed out — but she wouldn't, would she?" Later he said: "Has it ever occurred to you that marriage is an accident?" And finally he added, "Well, this is the end."

This perturbation and bewilderment left him when he stepped before the altar to meet his bride; he was calm though pale, and he made his responses in a clear, firm voice. Catharine Bosworth, in the lace veil and the wedding gown which had been worn by her mother and her great-grandmother and had been altered only to fit a different figure, was a truly beautiful bride. When she cast back her veil and the united couple walked side by side down the aisle on the straight path of their married life they both seemed happy and relieved. The ensuing reception at the dwelling of Mrs. Penn Scott, the aunt of Catharine Bosworth, on Louisburg Square, was solemn, staid, and beautiful. The line of carriages driving to the house stretched well into Charles Street, and the fresh green leaves of June upon the streets around the Square were symbolically significant. The young couple stood by the rear windows of the great parlor, behind an enbankment of ferns, mosses, and wild flowers gathered by Elizabeth Apley's directions from Hillcrest in Milton; and thus George Apley and Catharine Bosworth were embarked on their new responsibility of marriage.

It may be added that marriage in those days was a more serious matter than it is at present, where the possibility of the breaking of ties may from the first be treated plausibly. At the time of George Apley's marriage such an eventuality was beyond even faint consideration, and this is the reason, as the author earnestly believes, that so much of the life of his period moved tranquilly without friction. Those concessions so necessary in the bond of matrimony were more readily arranged because, in a sense, they were inevitable.

It was Catharine Bosworth's wish to spend their two weeks' honeymoon at some point distant from Boston where both she and her husband might be intrigued by a change of scene. She had therefore selected the Narragansett House at Rye Beach, New Hampshire, and thither the young couple repaired. She could not have made a happier selection or one more temperamentally suited to them both.

The following is a letter written to the author by George Apley at this time.

Dear old Will:

Thank you very much for everything. I am feeling like an old married man already. Though the Narragansett House is rather "swell" it is at the same time comfortable. I am a little glad and I think Catharine is, too, to be such a long way from friends. Hardly anyone here knows us and though Portsmouth is near by, Portsmouth is not as closely knit as Boston. I have a sense of great freedom looking at the sea. Catharine says we never really knew each other until we came here, and I am inclined to agree with her. In the morning we generally go for a long walk whether it is raining or not. In the afternoon we drive, although the local livery is very expensive considering what they give us. At teatime we read Whittier and his descriptions of this part of the country chime in very well with our mood. In the evening when Catharine is not busy writing "thank-you" notes for our presents I read to her out of Emerson, while she starts crocheting a bedspread. This consists of a number of squares which she will eventually sew together. She needs a hundred and sixty of these squares and has finished eight. When I told her it would take a long time to finish she said that there would be a long time to finish it in, and I daresay she is right.

We are moving to Mulberry Beach next week. Catharine's mother has been through a number of old trunks in the attic, looking for curtains. She found there some of her grandmother's brocade curtains, which Mrs. Bosworth had entirely forgotten. They were better than the ones she had intended to give us but as she had forgotten them entirely, she decided to give them to us at any rate. You see, Mr. and Mrs. Bosworth came yesterday and are now staying with us at the Narragansett House. Catharine is pleased, because two weeks alone is rather a long time. . . .

Willing is Whitey's brother in the fraternity of storytellers. He is better educated, to be sure, and suffers also from the handicap of a native intelligence and instinctive good judgment far superior to Whitey's; Whitey's obtuseness is as natural to him as breathing, but Willing has to work at his, overcoming by sheer determination the plain testimony of his own observations and intellect.

From what preceded the account of Apley's betrothal and marriage to Catharine Bosworth, the reader has learned that Willing's description of him as "a 'man's man'" is in objective terms a blatant falsehood. It is apposite only in the subjective (and denotatively contradictory) sense attached to the term by Willing and others of his class who have knuckled under to the wishes of the elders on matters that self-respecting men and women reserve for their own judgment. The marriage to Catharine, seen by Willing as "very satisfactorily" completing Apley's development into "a woman's man as well," is merely the next stage in his subjugation, the *coup de grâce* swiftly administered to foreclose the possibility that he may suffer a recovery of his more sensual instincts, and, relapsing, entertain again the preposterous notion of marrying a woman that he actually likes.

The barrage of steely letters to Apley from the elders makes it evident that he is on no account to construe his union with Catharine as anything more fleshly passionate than a dignified merger of long-prospering family firms. No sooner has he accepted the bit and bridle than he is directed to the stalls he will occupy in summer and in winter on the families' breeding grounds. Catharine's mother furnishes the details of what he may expect in the way of privacy with his new bride; her father with ferrous delicacy honors the Brahmin version of dower and curtesy on the condition that his approval of Apley's accession to possession of Catharine shall not be taken as a permit to remove her from her family's control. Apley's father, Thomas, proves dourly reliable in execution of the punishment/reward alternative he had employed to scotch the ghost of the temptress-colleen; since George is now bent on doing what Thomas considers the Right Thing, George will get his financial security, regardless of whether he likes it or fully perceives how it is destined to indenture him. George's mother, Elizabeth, applies the finishing coat of semigloss varnish to the wooden occasion, in her turn making it as clear to Catharine as Mrs. Bosworth did for George that the bride is not to misinterpret her impending nuptials as an emancipation, but rather as a more demanding form of servitude.

Willing strenuously misrepresents the whole exercise, using the language quite as shamelessly as Humpty Dumpty did ("When *I* use a word, it means just what I choose it to mean—neither more nor less") but without admitting it. Selfishness is unctuously praised as generosity. Meddlesomeness becomes "interest" and tyranny travels under the names of "solicitude" and "devotion." The only correspondent who calls things by their right names is maverick Uncle Horatio, and even he is sufficiently circumspect about this perfectly dreadful ordeal to escape with no more than a hint of rebuke from Willing. No wonder Willing artlessly confides that it was not unknown for young Bostonians, finding themselves in Apley's position of being harnessed and yoked, to take to their heels, never to be heard or spoken of again. And no wonder: when the prospect of impending marriage becomes barely tolerable only after one's friends have collaborated in getting all involved roaring drunk, with potentially fatal consequences; one's in-laws feel heartily free to horn in on the wedding trip; and one's new spouse greets their arrival as a welcome relief from the prospect of two weeks in the exclusive company of her mate, it is difficult to imagine how any sane person could contemplate the experience without feeling a kinship with a man going to be hanged.

For the writer-in-training, the usefulness of *Apley* (and Marquand's other first-rate work: *Wickford Point, H. M. Pulham, Esq.*, and perhaps *B. F.'s Daughter*) is the example that it offers in authorial self-restraint. The scribbler's obligation when writing about characters whose conduct is comical is precisely the same as his obligation when writing about characters whose behavior is reprehensible: present the data without authorial comment, and have the decency to allow the reader to interpret the facts for himself. Adult readers think of themselves as people with working intellects, prepared by education and experience to form their own conclusions. They can be a cantankerous lot, impatient when preached at, but in one significant respect they are reliable: they treasure what they discover for themselves, and gravitate toward writers who honor their ambitions to reckon on their own.

8

Writers really take their worst shellacking from other writers. . . .

–E. B. White to John Updike, December 11, 1971

White was of course correct; Rex Stout had said in a newspaper interview that Updike was "being pretentious with the title Redux and although my [White's] stuff didn't amount to much I [he] never made a mistake." And writers also engage in a good deal of self-flagellation, whipping the creative scourge back and forth over their naked brains because the damned things that they're working on aren't going right and they're stuck, and it can't be anyone else's fault so it must be their own. But though White was on the money about the usual sources of the nastiest public shellackings, and if what we do to ourselves doesn't count in the pounding department, there can't be too much question that the most numerous, though only semipublic discouragements issue from the nature of the industry itself, and the people we encounter when we try to publish our work.

That is the subject of the next and last chapter, and it is fairly depressing. So it seems appropriate here to refresh our recollections about just what it is that makes people want to be writers at all, and want it badly enough to undertake all the hard work in order to risk the rebuffs.

Our post-World War II generations represent the products of a sea change in the attitude that Western nations have taken toward higher education. Malcolm Cowley, reflecting on the work of American writers living in the Paris of the twenties, said that the city and the war that had culturally beached so many of them there had served as their universities. It all worked out pretty well indeed, but it was not the choice of many young people, or their parents, either, at the end of World War II. General George C. Marshall's plan for the economic reconstruction of Western Europe gets most of the attention in the histories of those times, but the GI Bill, making college available free to anyone who'd served, and wanted it, most likely had the longer-lasting effects upon our culture—if not upon our economy, and I wouldn't concede that point either—at home. Even today, four and a half decades after the war, the rallying cry of educators and politicians in the U.S. is that higher education should be available, though not by any means at no charge, to anyone who wants it and has the talent to go get it. That conviction would not be voiced if the majority did not endorse it, still (we will leave graciously to another day, another forum, and other panelists, the question of how many of those thus admitted to college actually emerge from it intellectually improved).

What can be said with fair confidence is that this general transformation of society has predictably caused a shift in the experience of most of the people writing about it now. It is not by any means impossible, but it is pretty hard, to encounter a new writer today who has not had at least some sub-

196

stantial higher education. And, given the monstrous dominance of family time by television since the early sixties, it is pretty hard to locate one whose interest in the lonely trade was not mostly whetted in school. School is where most contemporary writers chiefly developed their love of reading, that necessary prerequisite for the then burgeoning desire to write.

A lot of us wonder now how on the earth the first sparks of that love survived the drenchings that they received at the hands of so many grim enforcers of dreadful—but official— reading lists. My own guess is that once you discover that there are books and stories that delight, and that there really is no danger of ever running out (this can lead to concomitant mourning that none of us will ever live long enough to get through them all), no one ever afterward, no matter how determined, can ever talk you out of it. And so, ever after, regardless of how many sedative but assigned novels you plowed through, no matter how many dull textbooks caused you suffering, no matter how many charts and how many tables you tried to memorize, always lurking at the back of your head was the warm and reassuring secret that as soon as you finished your chores, you'd find something good to read.

I was not under any illusions when I resigned from the Associated Press to attend law school. I knew it would be dull (and it was), and that the massive study it required would cut deeply into my freedom, enjoyed for but two short years, to read anything I chose (and it did). But I also knew that when the mind screams out for some relief, a diligent search will unearth something. Surely not *everything* written about the law and lawyers is wearisome. Surely there is some surcease for the flagging spirit.

There was, and there is. Among other unrequired readings Anthony Lewis's *Gideon's Trumpet* (1964), the true story of how a janitor named Clarence Earl Gideon extended the *Miranda* rights (to remain silent, and so forth) to every arrested citizen, stands out to this day. But for reasons of the symmetry of this particular enterprise, I think it best to choose from Catherine Drinker Bowen's *Yankee from Olympus,* her biography of Oliver Wendell Holmes, Jr., first published by Little, Brown in 1945. This is because though she exhaustively researched the biography, and did her level best to make sure her stories were factual, she deliberately printed one that she did not herself believe, and so stated in the footnote numbered 3 at the end of this selection, "Holmes's last dissent. He resigns from the Court. A nation's greeting."

When Court opened for the autumn term, Chief Justice Taft looked at his brethren with an anxious eye. Old age, it seemed, had in no way modified Holmes's wrong-headedness; he still read the Fourteenth Amendment the way Brandeis read it, and he was almost a fanatic on the subject of free speech. There were, luckily, five to steady the boat: Van Devanter, McReynolds, Sutherland, Butler, and Sanford. But "Brandeis," Taft remarked, that December of 1929, "is hopeless, as Holmes is, as Stone is."

By all the laws of nature, Holmes should retire. As the New Year approached, newspapermen came round with the usual question. Taft read Holmes's reply and was not comforted. "I shall not resign or retire," Holmes had said stoutly, "until the Almighty Himself requests it."

But the Almighty saw fit to request—and suddenly—a quite different retirement. On Holmes's eighty-ninth birthday, March 8, 1930, Taft himself died, aged seventy-three.

The President appointed Hughes Chief Justice. Coming back to Court after fourteen years, Hughes watched Justice Holmes a trifle apprehensively. Was a man of eighty-nine capable of a full day's work in this most exacting job? Lately, Holmes's legs had become very weak. On that first day, Hughes noted how Brandeis helped him to his seat.

The first lawyer stood up. Holmes took out his notebook, unlocked it, slipped the key in his pocket and began to write. The Chief Justice smiled; he had forgotten this old trick of Holmes's. At the lunch hour he asked to see the notebook. . . . Holmes had not missed a detail. It was a perfect synopsis.

But after lunch when the Justices were in their places and the lawyer had talked for ten minutes, Holmes put his fingers to his forehead and went off to sleep. Hughes reached out cautiously, poked him in the leg. Holmes sat up. "Jesus Christ!" he said loudly, and the Courtroom stirred. Later that afternoon, McReynolds interrupted a lawyer who was young and obviously inexperienced. Holmes took his hand from his forehead and leaned forward. "I wouldn't answer that question if I were you," he said clearly to the young man, and went back to sleep.

In May, Holmes got ready a dissent that would sum up what he had tried to say so often concerning the rights of the states to make their own economic experiments. This was a tax case—the third in rapid succession where a man's heirs balked at paying a transfer tax on bonds moved across the state line. In all three cases McReynolds, speaking for the Court, said it was a violation of the Fourteenth Amendment for a man to be taxed in two states on transferred securities, and in all three cases Holmes dissented.

Preparing his dissent in the last case—*Baldwin* v. *Missouri*—Holmes talked about it to his secretary. Of course it was disagreeable for a bond owner to be taxed in two places at once, and he would say so in Court. But why did men make such an infernal fuss over these things? With taxes a man buys civilization—by no means a bad bargain.

If Missouri wanted to levy this particular kind of tax, Holmes saw nothing in the Constitution to prevent it. In nullifying these state taxes the Court, it seemed to him, acted on their own economic theories—and then called upon the Constitution as a sanction. Holmes had already stated his views briefly in the first two cases.[1] But there was more to say and he intended to say it:—

"I have not yet adequately expressed," he began on that day of May 26, "the more than anxiety that I feel at the ever increasing scope given to the Fourteenth Amendment in cutting down what I believe to be the constitutional rights of the States. As the decisions now stand, I see hardly any limit but the sky to the invalidating of those rights if they happen to strike a majority of this Court as for any reason undesirable. . . ."

No limit but the sky. The phrase caught the nation's ear. The *New Republic* said no graver words had been spoken on the Supreme Court since Justice Curtis read his dissent in the Dred Scott case. The *Baltimore Sun* said Holmes had given an "inside spanking" to a Court that was far too concerned with property rights. The *Chicago Daily News,* the *New York World,* the *Milwaukee Journal,* applauded this judicial prod in the ribs of a property-conscious Bench. Holmes's picture was printed, showing him walking to work on his eighty-ninth birthday. "Alert Justice Holmes," the caption read.

Holmes saw it. *Alert*—that was how he felt himself; it was good to know he was not deceived. The phrase was more reassuring somehow than any compliment to his intellectual powers or that "legal acumen" the papers loved to talk about. . . . Standing before the hall mirror on a fine afternoon late in May, Holmes looked at his reflection. His light gray suit fitted him nicely, the Legion button looked well on it too. He put on his gray fedora with the wide black band and stepped back . . . This was a better effect than that portrait hanging so impressively in the library at the Law School. Charles Hopkinson had painted it—full length in judicial robes, crowned with white hair and mustache. "That isn't me," Holmes had said when it was finished, "but it's a damn good thing for people to think it is."

HOLMES'S NINETIETH BIRTHDAY—March 8, 1931—fell on a Sunday. The newspapers greeted him warmly. "He is one of us, and few people can say that of such a man. He is part of all our past. It is hard to think of a future that he will not share."

Sitting in his library, Holmes read his birthday messages. From England came notice that he had been made a member of the Honorable Society of Lincoln's Inn—the first time the Benchers had elected anyone outside the British Empire. The *Harvard Law Review* for that month was dedicated to him. The Lord High Chancellor and the Attorney-General of Great Britain had written in it; so had Pollock, Chief Justice Hughes, and Roscoe Pound. Frankfurter came down from Harvard, in his hand a new book entitled *Mr. Justice Holmes,* filled with articles about him by such men as Cardozo, John Dewey, Professor Wigmore, Walter Lippmann, Judge Learned Hand. Frankfurter himself had an article in it. Holmes turned the pages slowly as Frankfurter, beaming with pleasure, stood before him.

Holmes looked up, trying to joke it all away, but could not, and wept a little instead at the tone of affection that lay so plainly beneath these public greetings. . . . Strange not to hear Fanny's voice, breaking in. *"Wendell! Your hair needs cutting. . . . Wendell, did you know the* New York Journal *thinks you are 'the laboring man's hope'?"* . . . So many to praise — but none, not one, to cut through with the sharp familiar voice that alone dares bring a man back to earth, back to the battle where he belongs while his powers endure. . . . *"Wendell—I see by the* Transcript *that if you keep on you may be almost as famous as your father, some day."*

That Sunday evening there was a microphone on Holmes's desk. At half-past ten, the President of the Bar Association and Dean Clark of the Yale Law School would speak from New York, Chief Justice Hughes from Washington. Holmes was to answer them briefly. The day before, the Associated Press had said the Justice would probably not use all his five minutes; he didn't like speeches and publicity. "But let everyone listen; this man is one of the few who make literature out of law."

Up in Cambridge, five hundred people gathered in Langdell Hall. There were speeches about Holmes, and reminiscences, until at last the room was silent, all faces turned to the microphone. The familiar voice came through, speaking slowly—a little tired but clear and articulate, rhythmic as always:—

In this symposium my part is only to sit in silence. To express one's feelings as the end draws near is too intimate a task.

But I may mention one thought that comes to me as a listener-in. The riders in a race do not stop short when they reach the goal. There is a little finishing canter before coming to a standstill. There is time to hear the kind voices of friends and to say to one's self: "The work is done." But just as one says that, the answer comes: "The race is over, but the work never is done while the power to work remains." The canter that brings you to a standstill need not be only coming to rest. It cannot be while you still live. For to live is to function. That is all there is in living.

And so I end with a line from a Latin poet who uttered the message more than fifteen hundred years ago:—

"Death plucks my ear and says, Live—I am coming."

Next day—Monday—the nation noted with pride that Justice Holmes was at his place on the Bench and delivered a majority opinion. All that spring he did not miss a day. To watch him was a miracle. "Justice Holmes," the papers said, "makes of old age a pleasure, something to look forward to."

But the people near him, the household, knew that his strength was very limited now—that he tired quickly and could no longer work at night. Next autumn, after the summer at Beverly, a great change was noticeable. Holmes was bent nearly double. In the afternoons after Court, Brandeis came round to go driving with him. They walked down the steps and across the pavement to the car, Brandeis on one side, Buckley on the other. "Straighten up there, Judge!" Buckley would say imploringly.

"You don't want to walk all bowed over like that." Together the two men tried to pull him straight. "It's not so easy as you think," Holmes said, cursing jovially.

On the morning of January 11, 1932, Holmes had a majority opinion to deliver—a case under the Prohibition Act: *James Dunn* v. *the United States*. In the robing room, Arthur Thomas, the tall, gray-haired Negro who had been Holmes's messenger for so long, helped him on with the heavy silk gown. The Justices entered the Courtroom, climbed the dais. Brandeis was not in Court that day. Chief Justice Hughes, holding tightly to Holmes's arm, felt him lean heavily, stagger a little.

When his time came, Holmes leaned forward, picked up the papers in *Dunn* v. *the United States*. Spectators noticed how well he looked; the cheeks were pink against the white hair and mustache. But when he began to read, Holmes's voice faltered, thickened. He shook his head impatiently and went on. But what he said was barely audible beyond the front row of benches.

At the noon recess, Holmes left the Courtroom with the other Justices, ate his box lunch and returned to the Bench. When Court rose at four-thirty, he got his hat and coat, walked over to the Clerk's desk. "I won't be down tomorrow," he said.

That night, Holmes wrote his resignation to the President . . . *The time has come and I bow to the inevitable. I have nothing but kindness to remember from you and from my brethren. My last word should be one of grateful thanks.*

It was Brandeis who missed him most. Next day at noon the Justices wrote to Holmes and sent the note around by messenger. Holmes sent back his reply:—

My Dear Brethren:

You must let me call you so once more. Your more than kind, your generous, letter, touches me to the bottom of my heart. The long and intimate association with men who so command my respect and admiration could not but fix my affection as well. For such little time as may be left for me I shall treasure it as adding gold to the sunset.

Affectionately yours,
OLIVER WENDELL HOLMES

Holmes's resignation left a solid conservative majority on the Bench. At such a time this was more than a misfortune, it was a disaster. The choice was in Hoover's hands—and in January, 1932, three years of depression had wiped out the nation's confidence in its President's ability to do anything right, let alone choose a liberal justice. The Senate had turned down Hoover's last appointee to the Court—Judge Parker of North Carolina; with protest they had accepted Hughes as Chief Justice.

What if Hoover put in Calvin Coolidge? His name was on the list. Or John W. Davis, or Rugg of Massachusetts? Republican insurgents like Senator Norris, Democratic Senators from Arkansas, Montana, Texas, issued statements that were half praise for the departed, half angry warning for the future. Holmes, of course, was a Republican. The actual party affiliations of the new Justice wouldn't matter; the history of the Supreme Court proved that. What mattered desperately was whether Hoover's appointee was going to vote down every reform Congress put through. In this worst financial panic of history, the nation turned to the government for relief, asked control over prices, credit, commerce. The demand, carrying more power and more desperation than any such popular demand before, bore almost the aspect of revolution.

The nation, in short, asked protection against a system that had let disaster come upon it. Newspapers ran angry editorials:—

> Government is at stake! The resignation of that noble old justice, Holmes, destroys a liberal majority of one. Let the U.S. Senate put Hoover's choice of that liberal majority of

one under a microscope—and fight to the last ditch for a new justice having the views—if not the legal acumen—of an Oliver Wendell Holmes!

Holmes read the reports, heard all over the nation the alarums sound—and was not afraid. Ninety years of living does not encourage a man to panic. People talked of revolution. An ugly word, a terrible word. Holmes had heard it before. Seventy years ago he had seen the country come through a revolution—they called it a Civil War. He had prophesied that not internal disputes but competition from new races would test whether our government "could hang together and could fight." He still believed it. There were plenty of things wrong with the United States Government and while free speech endured there would be, fortunately, plenty of people to stand up and shout about it. But Holmes believed the United States Government was strong and would endure. He had said so more than once.

As for his own immediate successor on the Court, he hoped it would be Cardozo. Not only was Cardozo's legal philosophy close to his own; the man's sensitiveness of perception, his generosity of view, were extraordinary. But it was not Holmes's business to make known his choice. He was out of it. He had resigned, retired.

SILENCE, RESIGNATION. To sit in one's library in the morning and read eulogies of oneself, receive admiring visitors. . . . Was there any praise, were there any crowns in heaven or earth to take the place of the work a man loved and had relinquished? In all his life, Holmes had never been without a job. At night the papers on his desk, the Year Book with the marker at the page—these had been for him the bridge between night and morning. The very act of waking each day had been exciting, with the battle waiting. *"Bugler, blow the charge! I am ready. . . ."*

And now the bugler blew his charge no more. The battle was over, the challenger was still. Holmes felt tired, exhausted.

When he tried to write his friends about his resignation, it was hard even to hold the pen.

Anxiously the household watched him. For the past ten years Dr. Adams,[2] the family physician, had said the Judge would die if he stopped work. Holmes, indeed, had said it himself. Now the prophecy seemed in danger of fulfillment.

But it was not fulfilled. For Holmes, fate had not reserved this particular defeat—to die of heartbreak because he was no longer useful. Three years of life remained, and they were not to be unhappy years. Once more Holmes rallied, once more his spirit reasserted itself.

It was to Pollock he gave testimony. It was "wonderful and incredible to have no duties"; he could not have believed how much he would like it. There was so much to learn! His secretary read aloud by the hour while Holmes played solitaire or sat listening. Often he seemed to doze, but if the secretary stopped reading, Holmes sat forward instantly. "What?" he would say. "What, Sonny?" And he would begin instantly to discuss the book. Just before they went to Beverly Farms, Holmes wrote to Pollock that he must surely be getting cultivated—his secretary calculated they had read 4,500,000 words! Spengler and John Dewey, Salter and Belloc and McDougall and C. D. Broad—"sweetened," Holmes said, by rereading all of Sherlock Holmes. He couldn't agree with Parrington and Beard that the American Constitution represented a triumph of the money power over democratic individualism. Belittling arguments always have a force of their own. "But you and I," Holmes added to Pollock, "believe that high-mindedness is not impossible to man."

Frankfurter came, one day, with the manuscript of a book about Brandeis, a companion volume to the one he had got out about Holmes. Would the Judge write an introduction? Very gladly, Holmes said. He had known Brandeis — how long? Why, it was half a century! Ever since the '70s when Brandeis emerged from the Law School to be Sam Warren's partner on

State Street. . . . "In moments of discouragement that we all pass through," Holmes wrote, "Brandeis always has had the happy word that lifts one's heart. It came from knowledge, experience, courage and the high way in which he has always taken life. Whenever he left my house I was likely to say to my wife, 'There goes a really good man.'"

Beverly that summer was beautiful. Fanny's rose garden bloomed riotously and his own patch of wild flowers seemed lovelier than ever. Old friends came out from Boston, bringing their grandchildren. Holmes enjoyed these young people. There was a singular and striking beauty now to Holmes's face, a quality almost luminous. Sitting on the porch he discussed life with Betsy Warder, aged sixteen. "I won't refrain from talking about anything because you're too young," Holmes told her, "if you won't because I'm too old."

In the fall when he returned to Washington, Frankfurter sent down a new secretary as usual. It would do the young men good, he said, to be with Holmes even if he was no longer on the Court. Holmes protested, but he was very glad to have a man in the house to talk to. The secretary, arriving in October, watched the Judge with amazement, particularly at breakfast. Why, the old man attacked his breakfast like a cavalry officer in the field! Porridge — a heaping plateful with thick cream, lots of sugar. Fruit, broiled fish, muffins, marmalade, coffee. After breakfast the Judge announced he was going to loaf all day. "Ninety-two has outlived duty," he said with what seemed a vast satisfaction. Half an hour later he was calling for the secretary to read to him. "Let's have a little self-improvement, Sonny."

Beyond all other traits, this perpetual thirst to learn surprised both young and old. Franklin D. Roosevelt, a few days after his inauguration in 1933, came round to call. He found Holmes in his library, reading Plato. The question rose irresistibly. "Why do you read Plato, Mr. Justice?"

"To improve my mind, Mr. President," Holmes replied.

It was true. *The rule of joy and the law of duty seem to me all one.* Years ago, Holmes had said it, and time had not disproved it. To the beholder there was something enormously reassuring in this spectacle of a man so old and so wise, who still desired to learn.

The morning the President called, Frankfurter was there, and Harold Laski. Three days earlier — March 5 — Roosevelt had closed the banks, laid an embargo on gold and called a special session of Congress for March ninth. March ninth was tomorrow. Tomorrow the President, standing before Congress, would present his plan for the national emergency.

Rising when his visit was ended, Roosevelt paused at the door, turned earnestly to Holmes and addressed him as the greatest living American. "You have lived through half our country's history; you have seen its great men. This is a dark hour. Justice Holmes, what is your advice to me?"

Holmes looked at him. "You are in a war, Mr. President," he said. "I was in a war, too. And in a war there is only one rule: *Form your battalions and fight.*"[3]

The footnote reads: "This story has been told many times. I include it because it is a recognized part of Holmes's history. But I don't like it. It is out of character. It smacks of the grandiose, and I suspect the witnesses of blowing it up because they loved the Justice. . . . 'Don't call me Hero!' Holmes said. . . ."

It seems pretty evident that it was chiefly the last paragraph of the short legend that bothered Mrs. Bowen (we have to make deductions now because everyone who could clarify the matter died years ago). But that really doesn't matter, for our purposes; what matters for the writer is the conundrum that she faced, its only possible creators FDR, Felix Frankfurter, and Harold Laski. Her manifest but charming irritation owed its stimulation to her conviction that at least one of them had fabricated that battle cry imputed to Holmes. And by implication: that none of the others present for the meeting was sufficiently exercised about that piece of embroidery to contradict it. But she evidently found nothing uncharacteristic in Holmes's reply to Roosevelt's inquiry for his motive in reading Plato (with its implied predicate "at your age?"); in order to include the first, trustworthy part she deemed herself constrained by the general knowledge of the story to include the second part as well, lest she be accused either of ignorance, or bowdlerizing history.

What we have here, then, is one of those stories that is so good the complete truth of it doesn't matter. That is the advantage for the fiction writer: he works free of the historian's obligation to warrant the authenticity of the words uttered or the actuality of the deeds committed by his characters; everything the fiction writer reports that his characters said and did is by definition what they said and what they did. The only duty for the fiction writer is to make sure that his reports will seem true; that the story is so good that its veracity is irrelevant.

That is the symmetry prompting the selection of Mrs. Bowen's work here. Gay Talese sought to employ the methods O'Hara and Shaw used to write fiction, to lend atmosphere to a report of facts. William Manchester scrupulously declared his reliance upon the methodology of fiction to render an account essentially factual, but substantially colored by emotions recollected in tranquillity. The stories that were so good we never bothered to challenge their factuality are the ones that made us love to read, and that is the reason we must write. An imperative of that strength ought to be sufficient to muster some endurance when the punishment mounts up.

9 If a young writer can refrain from writing, he shouldn't hesitate to do so.
–André Gide

The relationship between the student of writing and the teacher of writing has a lot in common with the relationship between the bagman and the politician he is bribing, or that between the horny single person and the equally horny, straying married lover. Each of the parties to any of the transactions knows very well that both of them are engaged in doing something that though commonly done is officially prohibited, promises more bliss in prospect than it ever delivers in fact, is invariably transitory, and more often than not ends by leaving at least one of the participants bitterly disappointed, the other permanently afraid of treacherous betrayal. Therefore neither of the parties to such bouts of illicit recreation wishes the other ever to call it by its right name or utter any hint of its probable if not certain outcome, and both tacitly but energetically conspire to make it appear to be an enterprise either of no consequence at all or one of assured triumph. That way at least one and sometimes both can pretend at crucial points that both are in control, and will never be found out. This seldom proves to be the case, but still, it's pretty to think.

Therefore to condemn this sort of conduct as deceit by mutual consent is not desirable, even though that is precisely what it is. To do so would in fact be hateful, an exercise of meanness in the odious tradition of that vicious puritanism which relentlessly pursues all suspected of enjoying themselves, captures them, puts them to death, and battens on their flesh. Furthermore, denunciation would not be practical; this is a hard life, requiring some if only phantom surcease for survival, and since writing is about that very travail, specialization in it should provide its own painkillers.

The first object of the student of writing is consequently to play upon himself the same trick that he hopes to learn to play upon his readers, much as the physician seeking to become a psychiatrist must affirm his credence of the arcana of soothsaying by first undergoing therapy himself. If the student writer has a teacher, it is the teacher's task to collude in the procedure. Each of them must do his very best to keep a straight face, because the student must accomplish, if only intermittently, the suspension of his firm and justified disbelief that he will ever get his work published; chuckles, even if smothered and indulgent, will defeat his efforts. The duration of the intervals of resultant credulity must be long enough to permit him first to write his stories and then to vet them for submission, and second to package them for sending out to someone who will fairly shortly ship them back again. It is hard, as one prepares the self-addressed, stamped, return envelope, to maintain one's confidence that it will never be put to use, but that is exactly what must be done.

Many, when first venturing with grave misgivings to expose their work to strangers, find it surprisingly unhelpful to murmur as a kind of mantra to themselves all of the kind words and praise all their stories, and this one in particular, have won from lovers, family, and friends. This is the super-ego, up to its usual spoilsport mischief, doing its best to sabotage the fruition of all the painstaking work that the ego has accomplished under unremitting goading of the id, by making the host organism so fearful of public scorn and ridicule that it will never risk showing the story to anyone not under binding obligation to pronounce it good.

It is perfectly all right to surrender to that kind of attack, firmly resolving never to entrust what you have written to anyone who might be bold enough to tell you that it stinks. In fact, if the inclination to capitulation is overpowering, then it's probably the course that you should take. Confine the revelation of your work to those whose selfish interest —platonically friendly, carnally voracious, or familially benevolent—in your cheerfulness is hostage to your unstated threat to sulk and pout and become hostile if they should demean your prose, and if you play your cards right, you will never be dejected.

The trouble is that you won't get published, either. And do not get foxy here and start to scheme how to suck up to a lonely editor and make him or her a friend, or shack up with a love-starved publisher who'll swap print for ecstasies. In the first place, only a seriously disturbed person would sincerely wish to have an editor for a friend, and all editors know this; that is why they are chronically morose, neither have nor wish to have any friends, and if desperate to acquire them surely would not seek them in the ranks of the disturbed. Few are so disposed, and that is why they spend most of their so-called working hours "in conference" (preparing for lunch by ingesting three or four martinis), "at meetings" (having cassoulet or haggis washed down with nebuchadnezzars of inexpensive red wine), or "out of town at conventions" (doing the same things with other editors in remote locations where the climate and surroundings are superior to those where they are nominally employed). In the second place, there is only one form of stimulation that enables a publisher to achieve orgasm: that provided by *The New York Times* best-seller list reporting that for the twenty-sixth consecutive week, books offered by his house occupy the first five places in both fiction and nonfiction (and he will not groan in pleasure even then unless he got the lot of them for advances totaling no more than twenty thousand dollars, and allocated no more than fifteen hundred dollars to promote each book). Editors who antically decide they simply must have friends buy large golden retrievers, and spend their weekends donating blood and serving dinners to the homeless. Publishers in perplexing need of fulfillment peruse double-entry ledgers and vacation at resort hotels where the murals in the foyer depict Fort Knox and the Bureau of Engraving.

Furthermore, they are on to you before you ever leave the house. All editors and all publishers know very well that every single person approaching them with soft mewling cries of friendship or desire, or bold proclamations of undiscovered genius, will prove on the most cursory inspection to be either a degenerate charlatan or a pitiable buffoon who is willing to perform any unspeakable act whatsoever upon any animal, living or dead, before or with groups of up to ten, if it will gain for him sight-unseen acceptance of his manuscript. And they know something else, too, worse luck: they know that the person seeking such a deal does not himself believe that he can write, and is almost certainly correct. So, if you find yourself cringing cravenly beneath your superego's sneering as you bundle up your manuscript to send to unknown, unkind persons, you probably were best advised to save the string and wrapping paper and put the stamps to better use by mailing friendly letters to lonely and rejected serial killers doing multiple life sentences in far-off penitentiaries.

Convicted murderers, unlike editors and publishers, reduced at last to killing only time, have the leisure to pretend gratitude for your attentions, and nothing to be gained by replying that you sure are a lousy writer.

If on the other hand doleful prescience does not prevent you from sending out your stuff, you have not only reason to feel pleased with yourself, but a positive and urgent obligation to celebrate that pleasure. The obligation stems from your hard-won victory over your better judgment. That is a real milestone in this game. Nobody ever got started on a career as a writer by exercising good judgment, and no one ever will, either, so the sooner you break the habit of relying on yours, the faster you will advance. People with good judgment weigh the assurance of a comfortable living represented by the mariners' certificates that declare them masters of all ships, whether steam or sail, and masters of all oceans and all navigable rivers, and do not forsake such work in order to learn English and write books signed Joseph Conrad. People who have had hard lives but somehow found themselves fetched up in executive positions with prosperous West Coast oil firms do not drink and wench themselves out of such comfy billets in order in their middle age to write books as Raymond Chandler; that would be poor judgment. No one on the payroll of a New York newspaper would get drunk and chuck it all to become a free-lance writer, so there was no John O'Hara. When you have at last progressed to the junction that enforces the decision of whether to proceed further, by sending your stuff out, and refusing to remain a wistful urchin too afraid to beg, and you have sent the stuff, it is time to pause and rejoice.

The urgency of that celebration derives from the probability that your superego was right, and your work will come back, and you do not know when that will happen. You may get it back in a couple or three days, if the mails are working for a change and the first reader at the magazine or the publishing house was suffering from an unaccustomed bout of efficiency, a more than usually bad temper, or a violent episode of hatred for all who presume to write. Then again, six weeks may pass, maybe more, during which you will balance swelling premonitions that this must presage acceptance against sinking forebodings that no one's read it yet (either divination is possibly correct; the latter is the one that is far likelier).

When you get your story back, whether short or book-length, you will suffer several reactions so rapidly accumulating in your brain as to threaten psychic overload and shorting-out of your emotions. It may help to identify these before you experience them.

The initial response to the sight of your returning manuscript is a combination of rage and despair. The object of the anger is the nameless, faceless wretch who spurned your work. The despair is the product of your superego's audible gloating at your humiliation; it knew that you weren't good enough, and told you so, and now it's crowing over you and all your silly dreams. With any kind of luck, the despair lags but an instant behind the inception of the rage, so that your immediate impulse to arm yourself with an Uzi and pay a personal call upon the editor is quelled at once by your perception that a person so incompetent as you would surely miss the villain, and probably wound himself.

When you have regained some of your normal self-control, perhaps with the aid of your favorite recreational drug—I limit mine to nicotine, alcohol, and caffeine, inasmuch as I have always felt that writers need more potent mind-altering substances about as much as adult dolphins need swimming lessons; there is a point at which redundancy becomes ridiculous—you will experience a small surge of hope that the package containing your copy includes a thoughtful letter from an astute reader who admits to having torn out not only much of his hair but also large patches of his scalp in the agony of rejecting so fine a work, and offers humbly some minor suggestions that if heeded—a work of mere minutes —will transform your opus into a veritable masterpiece that no reader will ever forget. This is a valuable reaction, because it enables you to screw up your courage and cut open the package instead of using the knife on your wrists. It is not wise to go to the cutlery drawer until you are quite sure you have reached this stage.

The package will almost certainly contain what to a disinterested observer would appear to be your manuscript, in pretty much the same condition that you sent it. Your eye of course will fall as unerringly upon the wrinkles, folds, and dog-ears that the editor and postal workers insolently added as the pitiless gaze of an aging actress fixes on her first inchoate wattle, but the annoyance you begin to feel at this vandalism will be dissipated in a jiffy by the sight of the rejection slip or letter on the top—stories get slipped; books get lettered. In either event, it will not be handwritten, not even in part.

If it is a slip, it will probably be cheaply printed, either on a rough-cut from plainly recycled office memo paper or on a small oblong or rectangle that retains along the top edge visible traces of the mucilage employed to affix it to a pad of a thousand such greetings. It will not be addressed to you, nor will it in all likelihood carry any means of identifying the heartless sadist who dispatched it (these sadists are not stupid, either; they know about the Uzi urge, and prefer to take no chances that the author of this story actually owns one). Under the magazine's hallowed logo, usually smudged, it will read in its entirety approximately as follows: "Thank you for allowing us to consider your manuscript. We regret that it does not meet our needs at the present time."

The letter that comes back with a book-length manuscript (houses Torquemadian in their refinements of torture occasionally send the letter separately, first-class, so that the defenseless writer receives it well before the book, and undergoes a premature ejaculation of exultation that dries up as soon as he tears the envelope open and learns the horrid truth) is usually printed on a cheap piece of stock ten and one-half inches long by seven and a quarter inches wide. It carries the publisher's name and address (but no phone number that you might decide to try some night when you are deep in drink and anger, slurring hideous insults and fierce threats at the baffled handicapped people employed by the publisher's answering service). To the naked eye of a veteran reindeer herdsman in Labrador, it would appear to be a poor facsimile of the stationery favored by polished moguls on informal occasions requiring written expressions of good fellowship. It will be printed and will read in its entirety approximately as follows: "We are enclosing the manuscript you sent us" (unless it's coming later on). "While several of us agree that it shows promise, we are sorry to report that we have not been able to find a place for it on our upcoming lists, and cannot make an offer on it at this time. We hope you will show us any future work, and in the meantime, we wish you success in placing this work with a reputable publisher."

It is permissible to spend the ensuing evening wading around in the slough of despond, venting your spleen upon any persons who have been incautious enough to take up residence with you, kicking the hell out of the cat, and beating the daylights out of the liquor supply. The post offices are closed, and since the chances are that you determined when you sent the thing out in the first place to defy the snickering gods, and so refused to lay in a supply of postage and packaging materials sufficient to send it out again, you cannot do anything restoratively sensible until morning anyway. But when that morning comes, you must arise, hung over as you are, and ruthlessly force yourself to take whatever steps are necessary to send your story out again. If you see a parallel here between the painful process of learning to break wild horses and the process of becoming a published writer, you are catching on. The bronc-buster simply cannot allow a bone-headed, intransigent horse to break his spirit for him; he cannot spend the rest of his days slinking around the old corral, avoiding the contemptuous gaze of some dumb beast that has bested him only because it is bigger and stronger and meaner. He must instead, by the next day at the latest, remount the creature and show it who is boss, and if the animal wins that second contest, schedule still another rematch, and another after that, until one of them is so sore and worn-out that both know the struggle is over. Writing is the same sort of trade. The novice is outnumbered, as loners generally are, and has no way to certain knowledge that he is not good enough until he has been beaten so repeatedly and so severely that he cannot take it anymore, and gives it up for honest work.

The index of punishment sufficient to warrant abandonment of the struggle varies from individual to individual. A number of factors determine it: tolerance of pain and mental anguish (or a pathological appetite for it); intelligence (or the relative lack of it); degree of distraction by other unavoidable responsibilities (e.g., the necessity to earn a living by means of some form of time-consuming regular employment; claims and demands of loved ones and offspring); health; and in general what constitutes one's particular interpretation of Stephen Leacock's Rule: "There is an old motto that runs, 'If at first you don't succeed, try, try again.' This is nonsense. It ought to read, 'If at first you don't succeed, quit, quit at once.'" The issue for each person is the meaning of *at first;* in my case, *at first* temporally comprehended the years between 1955 and 1971, during which I turned out all those novels, each repeatedly rejected by publishers on both sides of the Atlantic, and dozens of short stories that led to fewer than ten publications, only two of which brought me as much as a hundred dollars, most of which paid nothing except copies of the publications. Since I finally got lucky, all that time and all that work are now classifiable by charitable onlookers as evidence of laudable determination. If I had not finally broken through, the time and the work (and most likely a good deal more of it) would be deemed by most estimates to have been foolishly wasted. The only person who can decide when the game is over and the writer has lost is the writer himself. When you think about it, that figures: he is the only person responsible for the decision to play it in the first place. If he did not win, well, most do not, and it is no disgrace.

Unfortunately the writer who proves lucky is likely to perceive that long-desired and hard-earned success through a personal lens that distorts the reality of what he has really accomplished. When you work very hard for a long time, alone, purely because you want to and with no promise whatsoever of assured reward, you tend to assume that because the task is prodigious and daunting, its successful completion must be universally accounted commensurately prodigious, so that when and if it is made public it will bring the kind of effusive accolades and vast rewards that attend large accomplishments in other lines of work. Unlike lawyers, engineers, teachers, physicians, and other more stable folk engaged in more common professional work, aspiring writers, when they envision success in their chosen field, presume that it will necessarily carry with it general fame and celebration, regardless of whether they happen to capture a Nobel Prize or any other writerly equivalent of the recognitions required to expand the fame of other toilers outside the bounds of their vocations. I suppose this is yet another manifestation of the antecedent narcissism that makes a person want to be a writer in the first place.

Not that it really matters, because cognizable fame almost never follows the writer's debut performance (and the few who do get it right speedily discover that they do not like it anywhere nearly as much as they had expected to). Most newly successful writers, having practiced modest remarks before their mirrors so as to be ready to acknowledge words of embarrassing flattery, find to their disappointment that there is virtually no call for them. Anticipated cordial dealings with the local authorized Mercedes dealer and the nice guy who runs the boatyard; long and liquid luncheons with respectful gentlemen from Hollywood; congenial, pampered stays at hotels where uncrowned heads of Europe dawdle; and most of all vast choruses of critical acclaim: these things seldom come to pass. What attends first publication is usually about the same resounding silence that attends the lawyer's first trial victory, the surgeon's first big operation, or any other pro's initiation to full membership in his occupational lodge; the unceasing hubbub of the great uncaring world proceeds quite unchanged from yesterday, unaffected by one's triumph and completely unaffected by the small cries of congratulation uttered by one's kith and kin.

When this happens to you, it will not be because the readers were repelled by your debut in *The Atlantic,* or yawned and put your book aside after reading thirty pages; they are not keeping silent in order to be polite. They just don't know about the coup that you've pulled off against overwhelming odds, and unless you make it your business to tell most of the people that you know about the current issue, or give them copies of the book, they will never know about it. As no one knew you wished to write, so no one will know you've written, and for the same depressing reason: no one asked you to do it, and no one cares what you have done.

The temptation is to blame the literary media for this cavalier disregard. It should be put down at once. The critics for the papers and the high-grade magazines contend with somewhere in the neighborhood of fifty thousand books per year, no more than five thousand of which will receive more than a moment's attention—and fewer than two thousand of that number will be noticed for review in even the most conscientious major newspapers.

Let me use the Boston *Globe* as an exemplar here: the most prosperous and powerful newspaper in the region of the country that almost certainly boasts more bookish types per capita than any other area of comparable size carries one daily review five or six days a week, and three or four longer essays on Sunday. Short takes and brief notes each Sabbath give desultory attention to perhaps twenty more. This is a good deal more space than the papers in Detroit, St. Louis, San Francisco, Dallas, San Diego, Cleveland, New Orleans, Philadelphia, Miami, Baltimore, and Atlanta—each a city with some cultural pretensions—see fit to devote to reviews of books; it is somewhat less than the Washington *Post, Newsday,* and the Los Angeles *Times* set aside, but along with them the *Globe* does not deign to compete seriously with *The New York Times* and its Sunday *Book Review* for dispositive authority on literary matters. Which in turn explains why the *NYTBR* enjoys that conclusive authority to make or break a book: no other paper seems to covet it.

Thirty books a week in the fifty-two weeks of the year yields comment allocated among about 1,660 books, apportioned among stories for children, detective fiction, science fiction, poetry, collections of essays, reference books, nonfiction works, and, of course, novels and story collections. If pure mathematical odds governed whether your book would receive consideration in such papers as the *Globe,* the odds would be nine-to-one against the book editor winnowing it from the flood of 50,000, and about three-to-one against its designation from the field of 5,000 as deserving printed greetings (these odds shift somewhat in your favor in your hometown paper when the publicity handouts shipped with review copies stress your origins, because all editors love the local angle—too bad all the other editors everywhere else regard that emphasis as reason to disregard the event).

Pure mathematics do not of course randomly control what gets reviewed and what goes ignored. If twelve dreadnoughts christened by the likes of Manchester, Updike, Leonard, Bellow, LeCarré, Halberstam, Mailer, Parker, King, McMurtry, Vidal, and Styron loom on the horizon for the month of Sundays that includes your book's appearance, you are most unlikely to find what you have written lavishly discussed. Your gravity of purpose and the freshness of your work may if you are lucky bump a Danielle Steele or Irving Wallace into "Notes in Passing," but when the heavy cruisers among well-respected authors show up at the same regatta, you risk getting swamped.

All of that should be remembered when by some quirk of the gods your book does get reviewed and the critic doesn't like it. Almost always your second reading of the ignorant fellow's condescending prose will satisfy you beyond peradventure of a doubt that he can neither think nor write, and has done you grave injustice. It is very hard to feel grateful for such notices, *and you should not try.* Astonishing as it may seem in the cold light of dispassionate intellect, my own experience and that of all—not some, but all—of the other writers that I know establishes that what seems to the author of a serious book to have been a superficial, stupid, and meretricious review of his work is almost always in actual fact a superficial, stupid, and meretricious essay drafted by a person who really did not understand the book.

This is not to dismiss all unfavorable comment as wrongheaded and unjust. Now and then a good writer fails to accomplish his ambitious plans, and produces a book that gets published even though it is regrettably imperfect because he's done his best and failed, and even that's still pretty good. Then it gets panned for precisely that reason, often indignantly. I do not know any practicing professional scribbler in such unhappy circumstances who has, after reflection upon unaccustomed negative reviews, refused to concede that the book did have serious flaws, and was not up to his standard. Usually there are mitigating explanations for the misfortune —personal problems, illness, deaths in the family, et cetera —but while they account for the regrettable result, they do not excuse it for the reader who's a stranger and paid twenty honest dollars for the imperfect work.

The point of all this is to warn the developing writer—and also to remind the conscientious reader of reviews—that while all readers to one degree or another must depend upon the judgment of literary editors and unknown critics to separate from the 50,000 titles published the 1,660 or so that constitute the year's inventory of worthwhile books (from which few but the most diligent reader will select more than 50, 0.1 percent of gross production), the events that follow acceptance of a manuscript are even more random, uncontrollable, and therefore more unpredictable than those that precede publication. The author whose first published work fails to deck him out in laurels should take the snubs with the best grace he can muster, because they may get worse when his second comes out, and his fourth and his tenth after that.

Now for the really bad news. The industry that annually makes available fifty thousand new books for the edification of some 245 million people in harsh reality markets all of them to a depressingly small minority (the estimates vary so greatly that I trust none of them; none reaches two percent of the general population). Fewer than five percent of the obstinate remnant that persists in visiting bookstores and gets cornered inside by interrogators armed with questionnaires admit to purchasing more than one hardcover book a year; only about half of them own up to reading more than one book during the preceding twelve months.

The figures tallied weekly by *The New York Times* to determine the thirty books—fifteen fiction, fifteen nonfiction— selling best in the United States for the previous period (the list is about two weeks behind the cashiers, so that a title appearing on the list for the first time on Sunday the fourteenth in fact began to fly off the shelves during the last week of the preceding month) imply additional reason for gloom among writers as yet unknown. By the mid-1980s there was little likelihood that any book selling fewer than forty thousand copies in its first month after publication would rank as an *NYTBR* best-seller. If my own experience is any guide, and I of course insist it is, that represents a quantum change in American purchasing and reading habits since the early 1970s. *The Friends of Eddie Coyle,* published in 1972, sold fewer than twenty-five thousand copies in its first *year* of publication, and rose as high as fifth on the list (then of ten). Now it would not reach the bottom of the newer, longer ladder, and books that I have published since, crowding thirty-five thousand only after several months in print, have caused not the slightest tremor on the lower rungs.

All of this pontification, and all of what went before it, is therefore meant to remind the aspiring writer and the avocational reader that the purpose of each of those complementary activities is to have the noblest kind of fun: the sense of the mind at play. The motive for reading, once you have completed as much formal education as you can afford or stomach, is not to satisfy any stern requirements enforced by any threat of public humiliation, but to participate (and not vicariously, either, but quite actively) in a performance of imagination and intellection that was not complete until someone opened it and read it. The primary purpose of writing fiction, and then publishing what you have written, is not merely to show off (although that impulsion precedes and contributes to the formulation of the purpose), but to entertain the first and second reader, the first reader being you and the second reader being every other person who ever comes alone to what you've written, and reads it just as you wrote it: ideally, by himself. If the first reader doesn't like it, the second reader will not; if the first reader is enchanted, then the second reader may be.

The secret remains that there is no secret. The way to determine whether you have talent is to rummage through your files and see if you have written anything; if you have, and quite a lot, then the chances are you have the talent to write more. If you haven't written anything, you do not have the talent because you don't want to write. Those who do can't help themselves. We do it for the hell of it, and those who raise a lot of hell, and then get very lucky, well, we make a living, too. There are worse ways to travel through this vale of tears than by doing the things you love, and making a living at it.

ABOUT THE AUTHOR

Author of sixteen novels, including *The Friends of Eddie Coyle*, *Outlaws*, and *Trust*, George V. Higgins has written three books of nonfiction in addition to the present work: *Style Vs. Substance*, *The Friends of Richard Nixon*, and *The Progress of the Seasons*.

Mr. Higgins practiced law in Massachusetts for nearly twenty years. His clients included Eldridge Cleaver and G. Gordon Liddy. He was Assistant Attorney General for the Commonwealth of Massachusetts from 1967 to 1970 and Assistant U.S. Attorney from 1970 to 1973.

A former AP correspondent, the author's varied and impressive writing career includes journalism for *The Atlantic*, *The New York Times Magazine*, *The Wall Street Journal*, and *The Boston Globe*.

George V. Higgins serves also as a professor of English at Boston University, where he teaches creative writing.